Kriegsmarine:
Admiral Raeder's Navy

To Ken?
With Best Wishes,
Joseph Gilbey

10 September 2006

Joseph Gilbey

Canadian Cataloguing in Publication Data

Gilbey, Joseph, 1928-
   Kriegsmarine : Admiral Raeder's navy : a broken dream / Joseph
Gilbey.

Includes bibliographical references and index.
ISBN 0-9685994-1-9

© 2005, Joseph Gilbey

1. Raeder, Erich, 1876-1960. 2. Germany. Kriegsmarine--History--20th
century. 3. World War, 1939-1945--Naval operations, German. 4.
Germany--History, Naval--20th century. I. Title. II. Title: Admiral
Raeder's navy.

VA513.G45 2005   359'.0092   C2005-906732-2

Joseph Gilbey
1 Elizabeth Street
Hillsburgh, Ontario, Canada N0B 1Z0
(519) 855-6126

www.grafspee.com

Contents

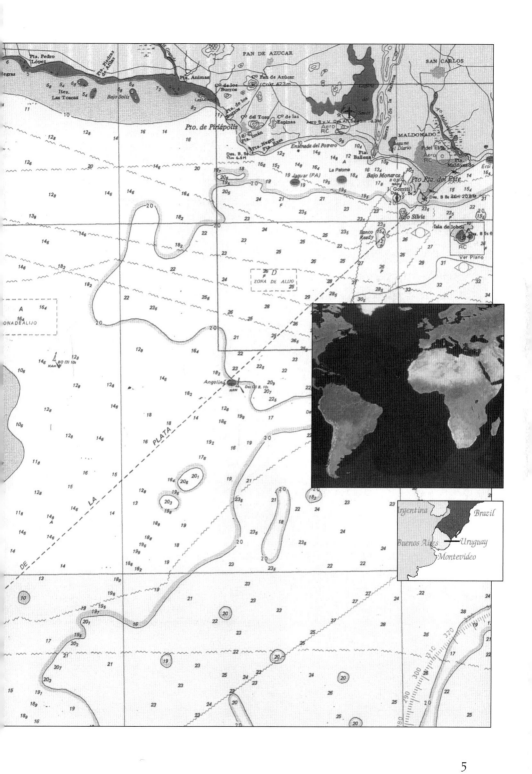

Acknowledgements

Many friends and associates helped in the compilation of this book. My thanks go to them for their generous contributions. I extend special thanks to:

F.W. Rasenack: A veteran officer of the German navy who served as artillery artificer on the *Graf Spee*. A loyal friend and mentor for many years, he guided and encouraged me in my research.

Captain Stephen Harwood R.N. (Rtd) and Captain Henry Harwood R.N. (Rtd.): Admiral Harwood's sons aided my initial research. They helped focus the text into a logical theme. I am deeply grateful for their assistance.

Professor Kieth W. Bird: Chancellor of Kentucky Community and Technical College Systems, USA, Professor Bird gave me access to his vast research material on Admiral Raeder. An accomplished historian and author, he will publish his next book in January 2006.

Diego Lascano: Provided many naval photographs to use in my work.

Mr. N. Joseph Potts: Improved the text with his editorial expertise.

Joseph Gilbey

Foreword

In Memory of Souls Lost at Sea

O Guns, fall silent till the dead men hear

    Above their heads the legions pressing on:

        (These fought their fight in time of bitter fear,
        And died not

           knowing how the day had gone.)

           John McCrae (The Anxious Dead)

Introduction

Adolf Hitler came into power in 1933 while Admiral Erich Raeder was chief of the Reichsmarine. Hitler authorized production of capital warships in 1937 to give Germany a powerful battle fleet. If completed, the Z-Plan would restore Germany's naval prestige that deteriorated in the First World War. Great Britain and France declared war on Nazi Germany in 1939 and demolished this dream. *'Kriegsmarine: Admiral Raeder's Navy'* outlines the history of the Z–Plan. The book records the fate of Germany's capital warships in the Second World War. *Bismarck, Tirpitz, Gneisenau, Scharnhorst, Lützow* (formerly *Deutschland*) and *Admiral Scheer* gave important service in the war. *Graf Zeppelin,* the aircraft carrier, remained unfinished. *Admiral Raeder's Navy* clearly resolves outstanding questions regarding the pocket battleship *Admiral Graf Spee.* Joseph Gilbey shows the history of the German navy, including the U-boat divisions, in a new perspective.

Author's Notes

Naval ranks: To simplify the text, German naval ranks in this book are translated into British royal navy equivalents.

Admiral Sir Henry H. Harwood KCB. OBE.

It is appropriate to address Admiral Harwood's career after his success in the Battle of the River Plate. In May 1942 he assumed responsibilities as C-in-C Mediterranean in place of Admiral Sir Andrew Cunningham. At this point, the royal navy had withdrawn all heavy ships from the Mediterranean basin. German bombers controlled the skies and the seas in the region.

Rear Admiral Harwood played his part in the defense of the Nile valley and the subsequent turn around of the tides of war. He gained the rank of Vice Admiral but fell victim to a massive heart attack in 1943. Following recuperation in England he became Flag Officer Commanding Orkneys and Shetland. Invalided from the Service in 1945, he gained Admiral's rank.

Admiral Harwood died on 9th June 1950. The navy paid tribute to Sir Henry at St. James Catholic Church in London.

A Sacred Cause.

CHAPTER 1

The Road to the Z-Plan.

Violent rumblings of social change in the 1930's rocked the status quo in many nations. Communism spread out of the turbulent Soviet Union. Fascism made its mark in Italy and in Spain. President Roosevelt's new deal in the United States drew strong support for the democratic republic while Great Britain struggled with upheavals in the Empire. In Germany an audacious leader drew strong public support and criticism. Some people believed Adolf Hitler would revive the German greatness of prior generations. Others feared the ex-army corporal's all consuming intensity. In 1933, the Führer of the Nazi Party became chancellor of Germany. The world would change irrevocably.

Chancellor Hitler's Nazi Party quickly asserted its political position. Hitler blamed the communists for setting a raging fire that burned down the *Reichstag* building on 27 February 1933. Next day, President Hindenburg signed a decree that restricted individual rights in freedom of expression and association. Immediately, the police rounded up and held many important communist organizers for questioning just in time to keep them from voting in the March elections.

The elections on 5 March gave the Nazi Party enough seats to form a majority - with the support of the German National Party (DVPD). Swiftly, on 23 March, they passed an 'enabling act'. All the German states lost some power and the Reich government gained unusual legal authority. At the end of March and the beginning of April they passed two more laws to 'coordinate the states and the Reich.' These handed Chancellor Hitler the power to assume a dictatorship. The Nazi Party now ruled Germany and Hitler ruled the Nazi Party. Ominously, an article in the Party newspaper *Voelkischer Beobachter* on 21 March reported a concentration camp designed to hold five thousand people. Local jails could not handle the Communists and dissidents that 'endangered' the Reich's security.

Hitler now held political power in Germany but the *Reichswehr* (Army) had the men and guns to enforce the law. Hitler needed their loyal support. President Hindenburg, tottering with old age and nearing death, still held legal power over Hitler's government. Initially, Hindenburg had scornfully refused to recognize the 'Nazi corporal' and his political accession. Now the valiant old soldier had succumbed to the euphoric nationalism that promised a new day for Germany. Hitler controlled considerable military force through his Party *Freikorps* (SA). Captain Ernst Röhm had built the SA into a large but unruly army of 15,000 trained men. He also had a loose association with other potent *Freicorps* units. Röhm, a very close friend of Hitler, wished to integrate the SA into the regular army. The army officers' corps firmly rejected such a move. Chancellor Hitler had to resolve this impasse.

Meanwhile, Admiral Erich Raeder, the *Reichsmarine* C-in-C since 1928, embraced the new regime. He believed that a strong hand would bring national unity. In his mind this was a prerequisite to his rapidly advancing fleet agenda. Admiral Raeder had inherited a 'sacred cause' to build a new German battle fleet to amend a disastrous loss of prestige in the First World War. Raeder had achieved outstanding progress in his mission. The navy expected to launch its third *Panzerschiffe* (pocket battleship) *Admiral Graf Spee* in late spring. Hitler had already approved an 'improved *Panzerschiff*' and the 1934 navy budget included another. Admiral Raeder planned to enlarge these two battleships according to ongoing international agreements. The admiral proposed 15-inch guns for them but Hitler fretted about a possible backlash from Britain. Finally the Führer restricted the armament to 11-inch guns since Versailles currently allowed this caliber.

In early April 1934, *Deutschland* practiced special maneuvers in the western Baltic. Hitler met a group of top military officers on board the pocket battleship. This group included Admiral Raeder, Field Marshal von Blomberg, and General von Fritsch. At a special meeting Hitler introduced his intention to merge the posts of Reich Chancellor and Reich President: Adolf Hitler would hold both positions. In return he promised to dismantle at least two thirds of the SA - his private army. In future only the *Reichwehr* would have authority to bear arms in Germany. Seizing the chance to rid the nation of these unruly storm troopers, Raeder and von Blomberg concurred immediately. General von Fritsch checked out Hitler's suggestion with his peers, then also approved.

Soon afterwards, on 30 June 1934, Adolf Hitler gave the nation an early example of his iron will and vicious use of power. Captain Röhm had angrily refused to stand down his Nazi *Freicorps*. Hitler met his old friend and argued for hours on the issue, but Röhm's mind was set - he would not retreat. Captain Röhm had 15,000 men under his orders and a loose association with other powerful *Freicorps* units. They had designs on replacing the Weimar republican government, using military force. On the other hand Hitler planned to use the political path to achieve the same end. Röhm left Hitler with only one route. The Führer immediately ordered a purge that opened the door to mass murder and eliminated Captain Röhm. Gestapo units killed Ernst Röhm and any other potentially troublesome opponents to Nazi rule. They summarily shot Gregor Strasser, General von Schleicher and many other 'unreliable' people. Reinhard Heydrich prepared a list of targets and Sepp Dietrich controlled the operation. Old grudges caused an overrun of the authorized list and more than 100 lives ended in legalized homicide. Josef Goebbels, Hitler's crafty propaganda minister, reported the Röhm purge. Goebbels blithely claimed the SA had planned an uprising against the government. President Hindenburg publicly applauded Hitler's firm handling of a 'dangerous situation'.

Coincidentally, when Sepp Dietrich's Gestapo thugs began their purge, the navy launched the third pocket battleship. On 30 June *Admiral Graf Spee* slipped flawlessly into the water at Wilhelmshaven. Huberta von Spee, Graf von Spee's daughter, did the honors. Soon after the purge, Hitler consolidated his dictatorship with a decree to combine the office of the Reich president and the Reich chancellor. A submissive 'cabinet' approved the decree. It would take effect when Hindenburg passed away. In August 1934, the 87-year-old president died. The Nazi Führer now reigned over Germany's future.

Meanwhile Hitler's foreign policy had progressed under the director of Joachim von Ribbentrop. The foreign secretary had pulled Germany out of the League of Nations in October 1933 and abandoned a Disarmament Conference in Geneva. In January 1934, Hitler signed a Non-Aggression Treaty with Poland. Afterwards, he turned toward Russia and cancelled the 1921 Treaty of Rapallo. This agreement had secured economic cooperation between Germany and Russia for many years.

In Berlin at this time Commander Hans Langsdorff worked in the ministry of the interior. Langsdorff's destiny with *Graf Spee* still slumbered in the future. Ordered to Berlin in 1931, Langsdorff had worked as naval liaison with General Groener's ministry of defense. When General von Schleicher replaced Groener in 1932 Langsdorff assumed adjutant duties. Von Schleicher's move into the chancellor's office coincided with Langsdorff's transfer to the ministry of the interior. Working in Wilhelm Frick's department had quickly disillusioned Langsdorff and he requested a return to seagoing duties. Newly promoted to junior captain, Langsdorff left his shore posting on 7 October 1935 and gratefully resumed his career at sea.

At the beginning of 1935 the Saar had overwhelmingly voted its return to the German Reich. Responding to a plebiscite in March, Hitler introduced conscription in Germany - totally in defiance of the Treaty of Versailles. Curiously, this made way for a naval agreement with Britain. John Simon, the British Foreign Secretary, and Anthony Eden met Hitler in Berlin on 6 March. The affable Führer offered the politicians an acceptable German warship building program. On 18 June 1935, they signed the Anglo-German Naval Treaty. Germany could now have 35% of British tonnage in capital ships. This agreement also removed submarines from the restricted list: the Treaty of Versailles lay crumpled in the dust.

Admiral Raeder's navy welcomed the new rules. They had already laid down two new 'improved *panzerschiffe*'. The naval dockyard at Wilhelmshaven had begun work on *Scharnhorst* in March. Two months later the Deutsche Werke in Kiel had laid down the keel plates of *Gneisenau*. Both these warships displaced 30,000 tons. The navy intended them to counter balance two new *Dunkerque* class French battleships. Meanwhile, Deutsche Werke had previously assembled six U-boats at Kiel and Raeder now added a legitimate submarine division to his plans. In September 1935, he chose Junior Captain Karl Dönitz to lead the first flotilla of three U-boats. Dönitz had just taken the light cruiser Emden on a worldwide training cruise.

Admiral Raeder's persistent promotion of a High Seas Fleet now began to pay dividends. The *Reichstag* approved a 15 inch-gun battleship - Bismarck - in the 1935 naval budget. The following year, in late 1936, they authorized another battleship - *Tirpitz*. Also, in January 1936, twelve U-boats joined the fleet under the command of newly promoted

Captain Karl Dönitz.

During a training cruise in June 1936, the pocket battleship *Graf Spee* called into Santa Cruz de Tenerife. General Franco, the governor of the Spanish Canary Islands, came aboard to talk with Admiral Boehm and Captain Patzig (Flag Captain). Franco claimed full support of the Spanish people in a planned coup against the Republican government. He requested German aircraft to transport his troops from Morocco to Spain. Admiral Boehm sent Franco's plea to the High Command. A month later - 18 July - the Spanish Civil War erupted. General Franco led his rebel army against a Communist controlled government.

Furious resistance soon catapulted Spain into chaos. The republican government declared a blockade against rebel-held ports. In August, a Spanish republican cruiser stopped the German freighter *Kamerun* at sea. Hitler readily approved Raeder's suggestion to send *Deutschland* and *Admiral Scheer* to protect German interests in the Mediterranean. About this time, Franco declared himself head of a new National Fascist Government. Although premature, Franco's unilateral declaration brought a supportive response from Germany and Italy. In contrast, Russia and France declared their continued support for the Communist Republicans. While these four major powers poured arms and aid into their chosen sides, Great Britain watched from the sidelines.

Providentially, 1936 brought major changes in British politics. Britain's King George V died in January. His son, Edward VIII, succeeded to the throne. The British people welcomed Edward's succession. However, a controversial relationship with an American woman caused the new British King to vacate the throne. Wallis Simpson had divorced one husband and now promised to divorce her present spouse to marry Edward. Some nebulous political undercurrents also stirred the mix. King Edward harbored fears of a Bolshevik eruption in Britain. Plus, with the exiled Kaiser's encouragement, Edward had shown a friendly inclination toward Hitler's Germany. Stanley Baldwin, Britain's prime minister, aggressively forced the issue on religious grounds. King Edward relinquished the crown to marry his sweetheart, 'Wally' Simpson. In December 1936 Edward's younger brother 'Bertie' succeeded to the throne. King George VI, a shy, uncomplicated man, soon won the hearts of the British people.

Meanwhile, Admiral Raeder's vigorous fleet agenda continued to produce powerful warships. On 4 October 1936, Field Marshal von Blomberg launched *Scharnhorst*. However, Raeder's growing optimism soon suffered a serious set-back. In a long speech to his top army generals on 5 November, the Führer called Britain and France 'odious enemies.' Raeder anxiously consulted Göring who assured him that Hitler was playing politics. They did not contemplate war with Britain. Hitler had constantly assured Admiral Raeder, after the naval treaty, that peace with Britain was a top priority. Notably, only France and Russia figured as potential enemies in Raeder's 1936 war games. They excluded Great Britain.

In 1937, *Admiral Graf Spee* stole the show at the Spithead Coronation Review. The compact pocket battleship with her massive 11-inch guns garnered good press and anxious reflections. According to German propaganda *Graf Spee* could run faster than a battleship with bigger guns and outgun a faster cruiser. Diesel engines could carry her half–way around the world without refueling. This information swept through concerned naval circles.

Eventually, Admiral Raeder's latent suspicions took material form. In May 1937, Hitler summoned Raeder to the chancellory and warned him to prepare for war with Britain. Hitler ordered the admiral to immediately increase warship production. This 'bombshell' gave Raeder the authority to construct the fleet of his dreams. Hitler again solemnly assured Raeder that he had several years - until 1946 - to get ready. Admiral Raeder looked forward to a new day of naval glory. Raeder's First World War experience had convinced him that the German navy, given an even chance, could match the British Royal Navy. The German C-in-C respected the ships and men of the royal navy and particularly admired Admiral Jellicoe. When the courteous British admiral died on 28 November 1935, Raeder ordered German naval flags flown at half-mast in mourning. Admiral von Trotha represented Germany at the admiral's funeral.

Daily reports from the Spanish Civil War now held international attention. World public opinion severely criticized German and Italian air attacks on republican towns. On 29 May 1937, republican planes bombed *Deutschland* off Ibiza. The surprise attack killed thirty-one German sailors and wounded seventy-eight others. In retaliation *Admiral Scheer* bombarded Almeria, leaving hundreds of people dead and thousands homeless. Admiral Raeder acclaimed the fearsome power of the pocket battleships' 11-inch guns.

The German navy chief now evaluated his choices in an expanded fleet. Should he develop a huge balanced fleet? What about a mixed fleet with fast cruisers and powerful battleships? Paradoxically, some important naval officers recommended a massive concentration on U-boats. Characteristically, Admiral Raeder gave the problem to a committee. Under the guidance of Vice Admiral Günther Gruse, a young commander inherited the task to prepare the plans. Commander Helmut Heye showed his first effort to the committee on 23 September. Plan-X suggested a huge balanced fleet that the construction admiral immediately knocked down. Rear Admiral Werner Fuchs said the German shipyards could not handle such ships and numbers. Anyway, Heye's sideline comment stated that the German Navy stood no chance of a major victory against the royal navy in this format. A second effort, Plan-Y, received scant viewing and a quick rejection. Heye's next submission, Plan-Z, offered two choices. The first suggested a mixture of pocket battleships, U-boats and surface raiders to raid commerce. This plan offered financial economy and fast achievement. Next came Raeder's preference, hard-hitting, speedy surface warships with battleship protection. Raeder carried the two Z-Plans to Hitler for a decision. The cagey admiral knew about Hitler's delight in the fearsome firepower of big battleships. It seemed logical the Führer would agree with Raeder's choice. Hitler approved the Z-Plan on 1 November 1937.

- 6 battleships with 16-inch guns @ 56,200 tons.
- 3 battle cruisers @ 32,300 tons.
- 2 aircraft carriers.
- 6 light cruisers with eight 5.9-inch guns.

Additional destroyers and future upgrading of *Scharnhorst* and *Gneisenau* from nine 11-inch guns to six 15-inch guns rounded out the Z-Plan. All of this would go on top of the existing fleet, including *Bismarck* and *Tirpitz*. Submarines, although included, took a secondary place in the Z-Plan. Admiral Raeder beamed with satisfaction, he could hardly contain his impatience for 1946 to roll around. The Z-Plan mirrored the new navy that the Kaiser, Prince Heinrich, Tirpitz, Scheer, et al had imagined in 1919. The list of approved warships meant the German navy would regain world class stature after the calamitous defeat in the First World War.

CHAPTER 2:

Kaiser Wilhelm's Dream:
The High Seas Fleet.

At the turn of the 19th century, an explosive expansion in maritime commerce resulted from the opening of the Suez Canal. Despite initial British opposition, the canal opened in 1869 to allow large ships easy passage between the Mediterranean and the Red Sea. A new chapter in trade between Europe and the Orient quickly emerged. Maritime nations rapidly built new ports, freighters and warships.

In 1897, Wilhelm II, King of Prussia and Emperor of Germany, attended the First Royal Review of the British Home Fleet. Great Britain staged a fabulous display of warships to honor the Diamond Jubilee of Queen Victoria. High on the masts and halyards of Her Majesty's mighty fleet bright bunting flew proudly. The Solent Estuary pulsated with festive spirit. Such impressive beauty and raw power proclaimed the 'Senior Service' as protector of the British Empire.

Wilhelm, a grandson of Queen Victoria, envied the undisputed sea power of the British Royal Navy. In this era, Germany claimed one of the world's best armies but she lacked a persuasive naval force. Kaiser Wilhelm had resolved to build a powerful navy to correct this situation swiftly. Admiral Alfred von Tirpitz, the Secretary of State of the German Navy, happily embraced the Kaiser's intention. Tirpitz planned to realize the Kaiser's dream of a global naval power. Four hundred million marks from the German treasury funded the ambitious plan.

Ten years of frantic construction soon produced twenty-two new heavy warships with six more on the way. Germany now commanded the third largest navy in the world. Great Britain and France nervously monitored the explosive expansion of the German navy. Britain intended keeping its present maritime advantage at any cost. Their naval strength equaled the power of the next two navies combined. Thus began a British warship building program that introduced the fearsome dreadnought battleships. France also rushed to augment her capital ships.

The First World War began in 1914. Germany now had thirty-seven battleships in operation and eleven more in production. The Kaiser's Imperial Navy ranked second in the world. Great Britain still led the field with sixty-six big ships in service and fourteen in progress. Third-place United States had thirty-one capital ships and five more building. Kaiser Wilhelm and Admiral von Tirpitz reveled in Germany's remarkable increase in sea power. Besides a huge increase in numbers, excellent quality prevailed in the German warships. Tirpitz strived to surpass the high standard of the British Royal Navy. He successfully drummed strict discipline and national pride into the fleet officers and crews.

At the end of August 1914, Germany's new navy faced its first deadly test. British warships staged a surprise attack at Heligoland. This tiny, rocky island in the North Sea rises steeply to 180 feet above sea level. It sits 15 miles off the mouths of four rivers. Germany had strongly fortified the island to protect her ports on the River Elbe and the fleet anchorages at Jade Bay. Heavy artillery installations gave solid defense from land approaches, while natural sand banks and shoals protected the western and southern sea approaches. In 1914, a minefield protected the eastern end of the Bight - a deep northeasterly access channel. German cruisers, destroyers and U-boats kept watch from behind the mine field and regularly patrolled the Bight.

The action began in the misty dawn on 28 August. HMS *Arethusa* (Commodore Tyrwhitt) and HMS *Fearless* led thirty-one destroyers (first and third flotilla) into the Bight. Three submarines of the eighth flotilla with Commodore Keyes in command supported Tyrwhitt's light cruisers. Five more 6-inch-gunned cruisers - HMS *Southampton* (Commodore Goodenough) with HMS *Lowestoft*, *Nottingham*, *Liverpool* and *Birmingham* - lay to seaward. They hoped to engage German warships running before the attacking destroyers. Swirling grey fog shrouded Tyrwhitt's strike force as he boldly entered the Bight: sailing into a trap. German Intelligence had alerted the defenses. Six German light cruisers were preparing to meet the British warships.

Raising steam at Wilhelmshaven - SMS *Köln, Mainz, Stettin, Danzig, Stralsund, Frauenlob* and *Ariadne* - all carried 6-inch guns. A consortium of destroyers and torpedo boats would join the light cruisers in a defensive counter attack. Lt-Cmdr. von Tirpitz, the admiral's son, served aboard SMS *Mainz*.

But unknown to the Germans, the British Admiralty had received early warning of the enemy cruiser deployment. They secretly ordered Admiral Beatty's First Battle Cruiser Squadron to Heligoland: HMS *Lion* (flagship), *Queen Mary* and *Princess Royal* (all mounting 13.5-inch guns) and the 12-inch-gunned HMS *New Zealand* - sailed under strict radio silence.

The Battle of the Bight ran for five bloodletting hours. German casualties numbered 712 dead, 149 wounded and 381 taken prisoner. *Köln, Mainz, Ariadne and the* destroyer *V187* went to the bottom. This initial sea battle marked a clear victory for the royal navy. Only one British cruiser and three destroyers suffered damage. Thirty-two British ratings lost their lives and fifty-five received wounds. Kaiser Wilhelm's bright image of a world-class fleet had dimmed when exposed to the awesome power of the royal navy. In a compulsive reaction to the loss of three light cruisers, the Kaiser decided to take personal control of his capital ships.

German fleet operations drifted inconclusively until November, when a victory off Coronel, Chile cheered the Kaiser. Vice Admiral Graf von Spee's East Asia Cruiser Squadron defeated a British battle squadron under the command of Rear Admiral Craddock. Von Spee sank the armored cruisers HMS *Good Hope* (flagship) and *Monmouth.* Yet this upturn in fortunes soon turned to gloom. Winston Churchill, first lord of the British Admiralty, and Lord Fisher, first sea lord vowed to avenge Craddock's loss. They rushed two new battle cruisers to the Falkland Islands. The battle fleet commanded by Admiral Sturdee brought von Spee's squadron to action.on 8 December 1914. In a running battle, the overwhelming British force sank *Scharnhorst, Gneisenau, Nuremberg,* and *Liepzig.* Vice Admiral Graf von Spee and his two sons, Otto and Heinrich, went down with their ships. *Dresden* escaped immediate destruction but HMS *Glasgow* later forced her to scuttle in Chilean waters. Losing two armored cruisers and three light cruisers made another large dent in the Kaiser's naval plans.

At this time, Rear Admiral Sir David Beatty commanded a powerful squadron of British battle cruisers. Germany's Rear Admiral Franz von Hipper also commanded a squadron of battle cruisers - albeit the German warships carried smaller guns. Providence brought these two warriors to close quarters several times during the war. Junior Captain Erich Raeder served at Admiral Hipper's side for five years. He became the admiral's chief of staff in 1917.

Smarting from the Falkland losses, the Kaiser ordered von Hipper's battle cruisers to bombard the English coast. To support Hipper, Admiral Friedrich von Ingenohl, C-in-C High Seas Fleet, brought out his battleships: but he cautiously assumed a central position in the North Sea. On 14 December, British intelligence alerted the Admiralty about Hipper's mission to bombard England. Admiral Jellicoe, C-in-C Grand Fleet, received the signal but it excluded any mention of German battleships. Consequently, Jellicoe ordered Beatty's battle cruisers to intercept Hipper's return to Germany. To support Beatty, Vice Admiral Sir George Warrender's Second Battle Squadron would sail from Scapa Flow at predawn on 16 December. None of the British fleet commanders knew about Ingenohl's battleships at sea.

In early morning mist Ingenohl's scouts spotted Warrender's advance ships. The German admiral incorrectly assumed that the Grand Fleet had sailed with an overpowering force. Kaiser Wilhelm had instructed him to avoid engaging heavy ships beyond the range of Heligoland's land-based guns. Admiral Ingenohl immediately broke away and steered for the protective screen.

Meanwhile, von Hipper shelled Scarborough, Whitby and Hartlepool on the English coast. At 11:00 he made way for home, expecting cover from the fleet battleships. Unknowingly, Hipper was heading for Beatty's intercepting battle cruisers and Warrender's battleships. At 11:25, Beatty and Hipper scouts made contact. However, Lt-Cmdr. Ralph Seymour, Beatty's flag lieutenant, sent a wrong signal that caused the British ships to break off. Visibility dropped to 2500 yards and Hipper's ships vanished into the covering mist.

The first months of the war quickly passed. Germany's High Seas Fleet wallowed in pessimism. Admiral Jellicoe's Grand Fleet held overwhelming superiority. German high command could not risk a frontal engagement. Public celebrations acclaimed heroic actions by commerce raiders on the high seas but the fleet lay stymied in home-based chores. Only von Hipper's battle cruisers provided occasional offensive action.

On 23 January 1915, Hipper led a scouting raid to Dogger Bank. At 17:45 the battle cruisers SMS *Seydlitz, Moltke, Derfflinger* and *Blücher* left the Jade Estuary. British intelligence gave early warning and Admiral

Beatty's battle cruisers moved to intercept Hipper. Next morning at 08:00, Beatty sighted the Germans off Dogger Bank. Thirsting for complete annihilation of von Hipper's squadron, he signaled at 10:47: "Close with the enemy as rapidly as possible, consistent with keeping all guns bearing." *Blücher* soon received crippling hits that slowed her speed. Then a submarine warning at 10:54 caused HMS *Lion* to turn 90 degrees to port: Admiral Beatty had spotted a periscope.

During the running battle, HMS *Lion* received serious damage. She lost speed and caused Beatty to transfer his flag. Falling behind his squadron, Beatty ordered the signal: "Attack the rear of the enemy." But *Lion's* flag lieutenant erroneously left a previous flag - course N.E. - flying besides the new signal. This ordered an attack on *Blücher* instead of her fleeing companions. Dutifully, the British squadron clustered around *Blücher* and pounded her to the bottom. When Beatty eventually transferred his broad pennant to *Princess Royal* at 12:20, he ordered the chase resumed. Too late! Von Hipper had disappeared.

Admiral Beatty later lamented: "The disappointment of that day is more than I can bear to think of. Everybody thinks it was a great success when in reality it was a terrible failure. I had made up my mind that we were going to get four, the lot, and four we ought to have got." In the Dogger Bank action Beatty's flag ship HMS *Lion* suffered major damage - requiring a tow to port - and ten British sailors lost their lives. Admiral von Hipper achieved another narrow escape, but losing *Blücher* with 870 casualties aggravated the Kaiser's growing unease.

Throughout 1915 and into 1916 both fleets adopted a stand-off strategy. Jellicoe's massive battle fleet lay in Scapa Flow ready to absorb any German breakout. The resultant 'fleet-in-being' policy effectively paralyzed both sides. Admiral Scheer, the newly appointed C-in-C of the High Seas Fleet, devised a plan to break the deadlock. Germany must force a redistribution of the British fleet and engage a splinter part.

German heavy ships began bombarding the English east coast - in broad daylight. British public wrath immediately demanded coastal protection. Lord Balfour, the new first lord of the Admiralty, suggested Admiral Jellicoe rearrange his fleet assignments. Jellicoe obliged with a reallocation of warships to protect the threatened English coast.

Admiral Scheer now planned to trap a segment of the British fleet. The adventurous admiral took aim at Rear Admiral Beatty's battle cruisers stationed at Rosyth. To alert British intelligence, Hipper's battle cruisers would brazenly steam toward Denmark in daylight. The enemy would probably send out Beatty's battle squadron to intercept Hipper. Scheer's High Seas Fleet, steaming a few hours behind Hipper, would catch Beatty in a trap. Rear Admiral Beatty's powerful squadron could not survive an engagement with the full German fleet. But British intelligence caught early warning of the Germans' High Seas Fleet preparations. Admiral Jellicoe ordered Beatty's battle cruisers to sea - steering toward Denmark. If they failed to contact the enemy, they would head north. Admiral Jellicoe's Grand Fleet, already at sea, would merge with Beatty as they steamed toward his position.

At Jutland - 31 May 1916 - the British Royal Navy met the German High Seas Fleet in head-on conflict. Beatty had sighted von Hipper's battle cruisers and immediately engaged. When his lookouts reported battleships on the horizon, the British admiral broke off. Beatty raced toward Admiral Jellicoe's oncoming force - not yet in sight. Hipper's battle cruisers and Scheer's battleships picked up the chase and soon met the Grand Fleet. Great battleships, cruisers and warships of every ilk - more than 250 ships - fiercely engaged. Jellicoe held the advantage in numbers and firepower but Scheer avoided massive losses with courageous seamanship and good luck. Early in the battle, Scheer withdrew his battle line - turning them 180 degrees in unison, destroyers covered the well-practiced move. Later, in a second withdrawal with the same tactic he required Hipper's battle cruisers to give additional coverage. British 15-inch shells battered the cruisers but did not divert them from their task. They took the Grand Fleet's best shots without flinching. After a break-off to westward, the German admiral had to pass the Grand Fleet to return home. Inadequate signals and extreme caution caused Jellicoe to position his forces too far south. Admiral Scheer ultimately fought through a light rear guard to reach home ports in Germany.

Great Britain lost six heavy ships and eight destroyers in the Battle of Jutland. Germany lost six large ships plus five destroyers. Counting both sides, 8,648 valiant sailors lost their lives. British casualties topped the Germans' because three battle cruisers - HMS *Queen Mary*, *Indefatigable* and *Invincible* - blew up when hit: cordite flashes invaded the powder magazines and caused devastating explosions.

Admiral Sir John Jellicoe received stinging criticism for failing to destroy the German fleet. In defence, he stressed the continuing superiority of the Grand Fleet. Jellicoe claimed reluctance to risk 'tenuous' actions when not assured of success. But many critics continued to pour venom on the redoubtable admiral.

Admiral Scheer's experience at Jutland convinced Kaiser Wilhelm that the Royal Navy outmatched his fleet. German warships had shown they could duel competitively with the British but he needed additional heavy ships. Germany's supreme commander hedged for extra time to expand his fleet. The 'fleet-in-being' strategy continued throughout the rest of the war. Predictably, holding the battleships in home ports without high seas action nurtured deterioration in ships and men. This fomented a disaster for the Imperial Fleet.

CHAPTER 3:
SIGINT: Churchill's Secret Weapon.

When the First World War began, Great Britain's Royal Navy ruled the high seas by a wide margin. Meanwhile, naval intelligence secretly worked toward communications interceptions. In August 1914 the cable ship *Telconia* raised and cut Germany's sea-bed telegraph cables. This forced the enemy to use wireless or foreign cables. By late 1914, British specialists secretly intercepted and decoded international wireless and cable signals. Naval operations received prior notice of secret enemy activities. Based in London, Signals' Interception (SIGINT) rapidly assumed a premier position in Britain's war effort.

Early in the war, an Admiralty wireless station delivered transcripts of some coded signals to Rear Admiral Sir Henry Oliver. The Director of Naval Intelligence (DNI) identified them as German. Within a few days the Marconi Company and the General Post Office added to his collection of such intercepts. When lunching with Sir Alfred Ewing, Director of Naval Education (DNE), Oliver asked him to study the coded messages. Sir Alfred, a fussy little Scot, loved dabbling in puzzles. A distinguished career as professor of engineering included an expert knowledge of radio-telegraphy.

Sir Alfred could not decipher enough of the ever increasing flow of intercepts: he requested assistance. The naval colleges at Dartmouth and Osborne supplied four language teachers - available during their summer holidays. Although competent linguists, the teachers had no knowledge of code breaking. However, an army code-breaking unit operated under Brigadier F.J.Anderson at the War Office. Sir Alfred sent two of his teachers, Alastair Denniston and W.H.Anstie, to liaise with the War Office. Recognizing the complexity of code-breaking, he recruited two mathematics teachers named Parish and Curtis from the naval colleges. Ewing achieved nothing except identifying the call signs of German stations. Then on 1 October, crypt-analysts in the French War Office cracked the German code used on the Western Front. They shared their success with their British allies. A flood of German military traffic immediately poured into the decrypting unit. Anderson's and Ewing's people busily shared the decoding task. Predictably, petty frictions soon arose between the army and the navy.

Sir Alfred Ewing now controlled six crypt-analysts: Professor J.B. Henderson (Greenwich Naval College) with Lord Herschell and R.D. Norton (Foreign Office) helped Parish, Curtis and Denniston. Three of these experts excelled in mathematics but knew no German. The other three knew German but lacked top level mathematics. None of the group had any experience in cryptography and lack of space in Ewing's office caused uncomfortable crowding. In October, the naval colleges reopened for the new academic year. Ewing now had to spend half his time away from the fledgling code unit. It was an inauspicious start for the most valuable British intelligence asset of the First World War.

Luckily, a trio of events quickly assured the decrypting unit's future. On 11 August 1914, an Australian boarding party in Melbourne seized a copy of the *Handelsverkehrsbuch* (HVB) from a German steamship. Germany used the HVB to contact merchantmen and the High Seas Fleet. Although the Australians overlooked the code book's importance, it reached the British Admiralty at the end of October. Meanwhile, a Russian naval attaché, talking to Churchill on 6 September, mentioned SMS *Magdeburg* wrecked in the Baltic. They had found a copy of the *Signalbuch der Kaiserlichen Marine* (SKM) in the wreckage. On 13 October, HMS *Theseus* secretly brought the cipher to Churchill and then First Sea Lord Prince Louis of Battenberg. However, the SKM code carried only weather reports and usually the Germans coded and re ciphered the signals. Nonetheless, Fleet Paymaster Charles J.E. Rotter, head of the German section in Naval Intelligence Department (NID) painstakingly broke the code.

Winston Churchill, First Lord of the Admiralty, instantly grasped the potential of signals' intelligence. On 8 November he composed an 'exclusively secret' memo initialed by himself and the newly appointed First Sea Lord, Admiral Jackie Fisher:

"An officer from the war staff, preferably from the Intelligence Division, should be selected to study all the decoded intercepts, not only current but past, and to compare them continually with what actually took place in

order to penetrate the German mind and movements and make reports. All these intercepts are to be written in a locked book with their decodes and all other copies burnt. All new messages are to be entered in the book and the book is only to be handled under instructions from the Chief of the Admiralty War Staff (COS). The Officer selected is for the present to do no other work. I shall be obliged if Sir Alfred Ewing will associate himself continuously with this work."

Good luck continued to help SIGINT. In November, a British fishing trawler landed a lead-lined chest in her nets. This relic from a sunken German destroyer contained a copy of the *Verkehrsbuch* (VKB). Professor Ewing's group now had the potential to decode most of Germany's military and naval signals.

At this juncture, the Admiralty promoted Admiral Oliver to Chief of Staff of the War Department (COS). Captain William Reginald Hall replaced Oliver as Director of Naval Intelligence (DNI). Captain Hall, a small tight-mouthed man with a balding pate, commanded the Battle Cruiser *HMS Queen Mary* before the war. Often favoring his personal judgement over regulations, he had ruffled many feathers in the Admiralty. Shortly after war began, poor health had forced him to relinquish his command. Captain Hall had a reflexive blink that evoked his nick name and emphasized the hard blue color of his eyes. 'Blinker' Hall quickly assumed his new post and discovered his natural element. Hall's brilliant intellect and heart of stone would shape British naval intelligence into an art form. He immediately arranged additional space for the crypt analysts in Ewing's cramped office. A small complex of rooms in the nearby Old Admiralty Building provided privacy and relative comfort. Known as Room 40, this became the code name for a top-secret signals interception and decoding unit. The DNI then appointed Commander Herbert W.W.Hope to analyze German intercepts. Commander Hope, although short of German language and cryptography, had outstanding knowledge of seamanship. He could supply naval expertise that the cryptographers lacked. Captain Hall wanted Hope to 'sift the messages and extract the juice'. Commander Hope's ability to understand the enemy's mind made his selection a stroke of genius.

German naval high command knew about the capture of the *Magdeburg* code book but decided to simply change the key. Every night the German squadrons and units radioed their positions. Commander Hope soon worked out their complete dispositions. When the Germans introduced a key change, they continued to send out many routine signals. Room 40 intercepted them, and this high volume of material helped resolve the new key.

Toward the end of 1914 Professor Ewing had five permanent staff members working in Room 40. Commander Hope analyzed decrypts and Paymaster Rotter broke the codes. Herschell, Denniston and Norton acted as 'watch standers'. They decoded, translated and logged new intercepts. Parish, Curtis and Professor Henderson continued as part-time 'watch standers' when not required for naval education. The network grew rapidly. Couriers brought a constant flow of intercepts to Room 40 from the telegraph office. In spring 1915, a pneumatic tube linked the office with Room 40. Ewing's 'watch standers' entered intelligible messages into the logbook and sent copies to Commander Hope, Captain Hall and Admiral Oliver. They logged but did not circulate unintelligible messages or fragments. The conscientious watch standers discarded nothing.

In time, a dispute arose between Professor Ewing and Captain Hall for control of Room 40. During the summer of 1915, Admiral Oliver (COS) gave Ewing official control but permitted Hall direct access. Although Commander Hope was operational head, he sought Hall's guidance rather than Ewing's. On 1 October Professor Ewing resigned as DNE to become Chancellor of Edinburgh University. Still, they prolonged Sir Alfred's penchant for hiring civilian intellectuals for Room 40 service. Ewing's old school, King's College, Cambridge, provided many controversial recruits. Alfred Dillwyn 'Dilly' Knox, a friend of economist John Maynard Keynes, claimed he cracked codes most easily in an atmosphere of soap and steam. 'Dilly' did some of his best work soaking in a bathtub. Ultimately, Room 40 contained the oddest collection of civilians ever to work in the Admiralty. Nevertheless, they provided the best naval intelligence in British history.

Before Room 40 became active, the Grand Fleet spent much time cautiously sweeping the North Sea for an enemy that it didn't find. But beginning in December 1914 no major movement by the High Seas Fleet escaped notice. On 14 December, Room 40 intercepted von Ingenohl's signal ordering Hipper's cruisers to bombard the English coast. Admiral

Oliver read his decrypt but overlooked the High Seas Fleet's participation. Oliver alerted Operations in this vein. Consequently, they ordered only enough force to deal with Hipper's battle cruisers. Beatty's battle cruisers from Rosyth and Warrender's battleships from Scapa Flow were deemed to suffice.

Winston Churchill, soaking in his bath at 08:30 on 16 December, received a rush message. German battle cruisers were bombarding Hartlepool. Churchill soon joined Lord Fisher and Admiral Oliver in the War Room to follow the action. However, Oliver's misreading of Room 40's decrypts had exposed Beatty and Warrender to the superior force of the German High Seas Fleet. Instead of Hipper facing annihilation, the situation was reversed. In the event, errors in judgment and communications annulled both prospects. German scouts contacted Warrender's vanguard in the morning and Ingenohl nervously headed for home. At 11:50 signals from Room 40 confirmed the High Seas Fleet's presence in the North Sea. Unaware that Warrender had scared off the Germans, Operations assumed that Ingenohl was advancing - not retreating. Fearing a surprise encounter in the mist they instructed the British squadrons: "The High Seas Fleet is out - do not go too far eastward." Meanwhile at 11:25 Beatty had contacted Hipper but lost him in the mist. At 13:00, Room 40 provided Hipper's 12:45 position, course and speed. This vital information lay dormant in the Admiralty for two hours. When it finally reached the British squadrons at sea, it was too late to catch Hipper before nightfall. At 15:45 Admiral Beatty abandoned the chase.

First Sea Lord Fisher was furious: "All concerned made a hash of it. The enemy escaped from the very jaws of death." Admiral Jellicoe also commented: "We had the opportunity of our lives." On the German side, von Tirpitz wrote: "Ingenohl had the fate of Germany in the palm of his hand. I boil with inward emotion whenever I think of it."

The British Naval Staff summarized Room 40's contribution in the controversial action. They recognized the failure to use Room 40's excellent intelligence. At the end of 1914 they stated: If Room 40 can decrypt the German signals they will forewarn the Admiralty of any major German move in the North Sea. The sources of information are evidently trustworthy.

On 23 January 1915, Room 40 offered another chance to seriously damage the Kaiser's navy. Admiral Sir Arthur Wilson and Admiral

Oliver burst into Churchill's room in the Admiralty. "First Lord" they cried, "These fellows are coming out again." "When?" asked Churchill. "Tonight" they replied. " We have just time to get Beatty there."

Unaware of British attention, Admiral Hipper's battle cruisers left the Jade Estuary at 17:45. Next morning at dawn, Churchill, Fisher and Oliver met in the Admiralty War Room. News arrived at 08:00 that Beatty had sighted the enemy off Dogger Bank. Silently they followed the course of events. Beatty's signal at 10:47, "Close with the enemy . . ." aroused great hopes. Soon the squadron lamed *Blücher* but at 10:54 Beatty believed he saw a periscope. He immediately ordered a 90-degree turn to port, placing his flagship astern of the enemy. But Room 40 signals had earlier reported the nearest enemy submarines hours away from the action. Failure to advise the squadron led Beatty to take evasive action from a nonexistent danger. Furthermore, his turn without explanation gave the impression he was breaking off. This caused confusion in his squadron.

Criticism for inadequate processing of Room 40 intelligence fell on Admiral Oliver. The COS handled an enormous workload, regularly sleeping overnight in the War Room and rarely leaving it by day. Oliver insisted on personally drafting all signals based on decrypts from Room 40. He accepted total responsibility and would not delegate any 'sensitive' traffic. Admiral Beatty complained, "Room 40 gives Oliver priceless information which he sits on until it is too late for the Sea Forces to take action. What it amounts to is the War Staff has developed into a one man show."

Careless intelligence processing also helped Admiral Scheer to escape serious losses at Jutland. Room 40 alerted the Admiralty about the High Seas Fleet's preparations on 30 May. Operations ordered Jellicoe's Grand Fleet and Beatty's battle cruisers to sea. The German and British fleets subsequently fought a furious battle. Late evening 31 May, the battle had ended. Admiral Oliver believed action would not resume until morning. Having missed sleep since the Grand Fleet put to sea, he went to bed. Captain A.F. Everett, naval secretary to the first lord, stood in Oliver's place. Captain Everett had no experience in SIGINT or German naval procedures. Incoming decrypts indicated Admiral Scheer's fleet steering for Horn Reef. Captain Everett missed the significance of the decrypted signals and filed them for later handling. Meanwhile, Admiral Jellicoe had surmised the German admiral would head toward

Heligoland - many miles southward. Consequently, Scheer had only to fight his way past Jellicoe's light rear guard to reach home.

Captain Hall realized that the Admiralty needed a procedural change to prevent repeating the errors arising at Jutland. Merely passing on decrypts did not serve the purpose. Hall suggested that Room 40 prepare intelligence reports, based on their experience of German signals. But Admiral Oliver remained unconvinced and obstinate.

At the end of the war, Room 40 again showed its worth. Admiral David Beatty had dreamed of a conclusive naval battle to extinguish all hope of a significant German navy. Some opportunities had come his way but even the main bout at Jutland had missed the mark. In the opposite corner, Admiral Scheer fervently believed in German naval honor. The High Seas Fleet must go down fighting. "An honorable battle by the fleet - even a fight to the death - will sow the seed of a new fleet. There can be no future for a fleet fettered by dishonorable peace."

On 29 October 1918, a stirring of the High Seas Fleet sent Beatty's pulse racing. Room 40's duty officer Francis Toye intercepted signals at 02:00 suggesting a sortie of the High Seas Fleet. Toye, with one year's service in SIGINT, reported his finding to Operations but they demanded a clear 'yes' or 'no' decision. About 04:00 Toye decided 'yes' and advised Operations accordingly. Captain Hall and his assistant Captain James joined Toye in Room 40. Close to 08:00 they intercepted a German signal "All officers on board flagship." Nothing followed - only complete silence. This was the first sign of the German naval mutiny that erupted at the end of the war. Scheer's passionate appeal to defend the honor of the navy failed to attract many of his sailors. Mutiny in various forms forced the cancellation of this final sortie. On 4 November 1918, the red flag of revolution flew at most German naval bases. Then the armistice on 11 November closed the door on Admiral Beatty's fond hopes.

Early mistrust of Room 40 lay in the Admiralty's own stuffy traditions. The 'Senior Service' did not welcome civilians 'meddling' in their affairs. Inexperience initially reinforced the admirals' prejudices. Newly recruited cryptographers made risible errors regarding naval terms and geography. However, Room 40 intelligence rapidly proved its worth. Soon the Admiralty welcomed all SIGINT information. Ultimately, SIGINT secretly intercepted coded traffic of friend and foe - including official and personal signals.

CHAPTER 4:
Politics Versus Submarines (1914-1918).

When war erupted in Europe in 1914, President Wilson immediately declared the United States neutral. On 6 August, he issued a note to the belligerents suggesting they comply with the 1909 Declaration of London. Deep in his psyche Theodore Wilson believed he could personally broker lasting peace. Throughout most of the war he clung tenaciously to this vocation.

In Germany, the United States's perception of the war created a fierce tussle within the hierarchy. Chancellor Bethmann-Holweg and Count von Bernstorff, German Ambassador in Washington, argued that United States neutrality helped Germany. The politicians respected the potential of American wartime production. To the contrary, the military chiefs expected a quick European land victory and shrugged aside the politicians' concerns. Swift military success in Europe would finesse any United States involvement. Field Marshal von Hindenburg, General Ludendorff and Secretary of the Navy von Tirpitz focused their energies on winning the war as quickly as possible. Wilhelm II, German Emperor and Supreme Commander, anticipated a short war with maximum benefits enshrined in a peace treaty. President Wilson and the Kaiser had opened personal correspondence that continued throughout the war.

After the Battle of the Bight - 28 August - Admiral von Tirpitz believed that fleet engagements could not force Britain to negotiate peace. He emphatically expressed his alternative strategy: "Setting the submarine against English trade offers the sole hope for wearing down England's economic life." The admiral publicly proposed 'unrestricted' submarine warfare to blockade Britain. Tirpitz's widely reported U-boat strategy - striking without warning - drew furious protests from the United States and other neutrals. They argued it violated the honor codes of the era. Powerful German politicians, unwilling to risk agitating the United States, strenuously opposed unrestricted use of submarines.

Germany at this time had twenty-eight U-boats in operations, including ten ocean going models. Great Britain, with thirty-six submarines, considered submarines as coastal vessels with little high seas significance. Nevertheless, German U-boats quickly made an impact in the sea war. On 22 September *U-9* sank three British armored cruisers off the Dutch coast. The German vessel torpedoed *HMS Cressy, Hogue* and *Aboukir* in the English Channel. More than fifty officers and fourteen hundred enlisted men lost their lives. Then on 27 October, HMS *Audacious* encountered a submarine-planted mine. The new battleship sank off the northwest coast of Ireland.

Great Britain unilaterally declared the North Sea a War Zone on 2 November. Tirpitz reacted angrily. In Berlin 14 December, he told United Press reporters that 'unrestricted' U-boat strikes would start on 1 February 1915. During his press interview Tirpitz mused: "What will America say if we open U-boat warfare against all ships sailing to England and starve it out?" adding quizzically "What will America do?"

Tirpitz's bold statements shocked Chancellor Bethmann-Holweg and his fellow politicians. Holweg anxiously exclaimed: "Publicly we warn the enemy to brace for an U-boat blockade. Publicly the German peoples' attention is drawn to their possession of an infallible weapon. From this point on, we cannot wrest U-boat warfare from the nation's soul."

German press reports jubilantly touted the navy's intentions but the New York *Tribune* found Tirpitz's threat incredible: "The German Navy and Merchant Marine are bottled up. Until British sea power is disposed of, for any German to think about starving Great Britain by submarine raids is fantastic." Nonetheless, the German navy planned for vigorous submarine warfare against merchant shipping. Submarine technology advanced and soon spawned U-boats that could penetrate the British blockade. As their range widened into the Atlantic the question again arose "What will America do?" This anxious question dominated German naval strategy and political thought.

As the war dragged on, political reality dampened earlier navy plans to move aggressively against North America. U-boat attacks off the American coast must not provoke the United States into war. The crucial factor remained America's tolerance to stress. Meanwhile, the United States experienced bothersome problems with her southern neighbor. Mexico at the turn of the century simmered in constant rebellion. Insurrection followed insurrection like the changing seasons. Three prominent political leaders wrestled for power but each failed to consolidate control. Bandit gangs led by Emilio Zapata and Pancho Villa added additional stress. In the background, German intelligence agents stirred the pot.

The Mexican President, Madera, publicly espoused democratic policies that President Wilson encouraged. Then a military coup abruptly ended Madera's administration. On 22 February 1913, General Huerta violently assumed the Presidency and 'someone unknown' assassinated Madera. Wilson suspected Huerta's involvement in Madera's death and denied the new Mexican administration diplomatic recognition. President Wilson's refusal to recognize Huerta upset some American tycoons who supported the powerful Mexican. British interests had also invested heavily in the oil industry at Tampico. The royal navy depended on Mexican oil for their new turbine engine technology.

President Huerta personally welcomed foreign investment. This venal situation infuriated Wilson who worked and prayed for a stable democratic system to calm the Mexican chaos. Unfortunately, many Mexicans regarded the American President's do-good initiatives as 'Yankee interference.' Finally, Wilson's rejection of Huerta led to an incident that shocked the world. USS *Dolphin* landed a small group of sailors at Tampico on 6 April 1914. A Mexican patrol arrested the sailors but quickly returned them to their ship, with profuse apologies. American Admiral Mayo was furious. The raging admiral demanded a 21-gun salute and punishment of the arresting officer for insulting the United States Navy. President Huerta, a proud full-blooded Aztec, refused to comply with Mayo's demands and ignored the threat of a United States ultimatum: Blockade and occupation of Veracruz would follow Mexico's noncompliance - the deadline to expire 19 April. Huerta shrugged and asked "How can I respond to a diplomatic note from a nation that does not recognize me?" Meanwhile, United States agents actively aided Huerta's prime opponent, General Carranza, to organize an insurrection. Contrarily, Germany had dispatched a freighter loaded with war weapons in support of President Huerta. *Ypringa*, carrying 200 machine guns and 15,000,000 cartridges now steamed toward Veracruz.

In the early morning 21 April 1914, President Wilson, Secretary of State Bryan, and Admiral Daniels conferred on the telephone. The United States' ultimatum to Huerta had run out; they must stop the inbound German arms shipment - somehow. Immediately after the call, Daniels signaled Admiral Fletcher in Veracruz to seize the customs house and prevent *Ypringa* from landing her cargo. American marines then invaded Veracruz and angry Mexicans resisted. Next day, USS *Prairie* shelled Veracruz. Nineteen Americans and 126 Mexicans lost their lives. An international backlash only strengthened Wilson's resolve to oust President Huerta. The angry American President blamed the Mexican leader for the calamity. Germany protested American interference with her sea commerce and received prompt apologies. Then they secretly sailed *Ypringa* into Puerto Mexico. A second freighter - *Bavaria* - carrying 1,800,000 rounds of ammunition and 8,327 rolls of barbed wire soon joined *Ypringa*. President Huerta's forces received both ships' cargos. If the European war expanded, German U-boat bases in Mexico might cause havoc to American shipping.

Far from the political arm-wrestling in Mexico, brutal trench warfare in Europe began with its ever-widening sea-war. On 25 January 1915, Germany added grain and flour to the contraband list. Britain promptly seized the American freighter *Wilhelmina* docked at Falmouth. Then on 4 February, Germany declared the seas around the British Isles a War Zone. They stated that after 18 February, U-boats would destroy enemy merchant vessels - possibly without warning. Germany opened this new phase of submarine war against merchant ships on 22 February but at the same time tried to avoid arousing American anger. British Prime Minister Asquith reacted swiftly and declared a full blockade against Germany. After 1 March, no neutral vessel could enter a German port or return from it freely. Thus, began the starvation tactics of the blockade.

American public opinion strongly supported President Wilson's neutral stand in the European war. Trade in war materials (entirely with Britain and its allies) continued to swell American bank accounts. The President piously stated in 1915, that the American people "demanded energetic words but would not endure energetic action." Wilson insisted that he would not take 'decisive action' without the full support of the American people. Working tirelessly to mediate a 'just peace', the president exchanged notes with the German Kaiser. They often discussed unrestricted submarine attacks. Wilson demanded that Germany respect America's rights on the high seas. Meanwhile, ex-president Theodore Roosevelt and his Democratic support group in the American east, opposed Wilson's neutrality policy. They pressed for America's immediate entry into the war against Germany.

At the beginning of May 1915, submarines sank *Gullflight* and *Nebraska*. U-boats attacked both American merchant ships without warning. Then on 7 May, *U-20* sank the British Liner *Lusitania* off Ireland. Newspaper advertisements had publicly warned that submarines might attack *Lusitania* if she carried war materials. Two torpedoes slammed into the liner and sent her to the bottom with 1,198 passengers - including 128 Americans. United States reaction overflowed in fury. News headlines clamored that Germany would paralyze American trade with the U-boat threat. War seemed imminent against Germany but Wilson would not budge from his neutral position. He stated, "There is such a thing as a man being too proud to fight."

President Wilson's rock-hard commitment to neutrality convinced Germany that he would endure anything to continue trading. Then a U-boat sank the liner *Arabic* on 19 August. Ambassador Bernstorff cabled from Washington that American rage had boiled over. Public opinion demanded a break of diplomatic relations with Germany. Chancellor Bethmann-Holweg lobbied the Kaiser to abandon unrestricted U-boat warfare. Admiral Tirpitz fiercely opposed Holweg. Political notes ping ponged across the Atlantic for days. Kaiser Wilhelm, the Supreme Commander, vacillated between both viewpoints. Finally, on 1 September the Kaiser assured Wilson, "Liners will not be sunk without warning and without safety measures for noncombatants - provided the liners do not try to escape or offer resistance." Germany then announced that sink-on-sight was off but it could only be a brief respite. Wilson also extracted a grudging apology and a promise of compensation for the American lives lost in the *Lusitania*. Still, vehement torrents of neutral complaints moved German planners toward a more acceptable use of U-boats. The navy developed a transatlantic submarine able to transport 500 tons of freight. This gave birth to a new freight service in an attempt to breach the blockade. On 8 November 1915, they set up Deutsche-Ozean-Rhederei. Alfred Lohmann, President of Bremen Chamber of Commerce, assumed the chair.

Germany launched *U-Deutschland* on 28 March 1916. Classified as a submarine freighter, she could transport 340 tons of deadweight cargo and 170 tons of rubber in her holds. The massive submarine could carry a further 230 tons of buoyant rubber between her pressure hull and outer skin. *U-Deutschland* displaced 1558 tons surfaced and had a range of 14,000 miles at 9.6 knots. Her sister ship - U-*Bremen* - also neared completion.

U-Deutschland left Wilhelmshaven on 14 June 1916, carrying dyestuffs, chemicals and pharmaceuticals to Baltimore. The huge U-boat made the crossing in 24 days. Then she loaded 350 tons of rubber, 343 tons of nickel, 83 tons of tin and 1/2 ton of jute sacks for the return voyage. On 2 August, the submarine-freighter slipped her lines and began the 22-day trip back to Bremen. At 15:00 on 23 August, she arrived with great fanfare into Bremerhaven. Following this success, on 25 August *U-Bremen* sailed secretly out of Germany, bound for New London. That was the last news of *U-Bremen*. She mysteriously disappeared into the vast oceans, never to signal or surface again.

In September, a new type of combat submarine-cruiser crossed the Atlantic. Under Lt-Cmdr Hans Rose, *U-53* had instructions to tie up in New London and allow selected visitors access to his ship. Hans Rose proudly displayed German submarine-cruiser technology, and within a few hours sailed out. He had orders to raid commerce outside the United States territorial limits. In December 1917, the Kaiser awarded Rose the '*Pour le Merité*' in recognition of his brilliant two-year career in *U-53*.

U-Deutschland returned to Baltimore on 1 November. She carried chemicals, precious stones and nine million dollars to boost Germany's credit rating. Outbound, she loaded twenty-three wagon-loads of essential materials and arrived on 10 December in the Weser. *U-Deutschland* then began refitting as a submarine-cruiser. Renamed *U-155*, she completed refitting on 10 February 1917.

Admiral von Holtzendorff, Chief of the German Admiralty Staff, had always favored unrestricted submarine warfare. Gradually, the politicians had urged him away from military imperatives toward the Hague Conventions. They argued that naval war was a means to an end and not a prime factor. However, adverse events had drawn Holtzendorff away from the 'Hague' philosophy toward the military route to success. Only U-boats promised victory in the sea war. The new hybrid U-cruiser aimed to fit both schools of thought. Admiral Holtzendorff pointed out mounting American military support of the enemy.

In June 1916, planning and construction of U-cruisers increased. On 22 December, the Kaiser issued a 'Top Priority' cabinet order creating a new U-cruiser squadron. Holtzendorff held nominal authority but the Kaiser made all command appointments. Also during 1916, Germany increased her fleet of ocean-going combat submarines from ten to one hundred eleven, including mine layers. U-boat captains then represented the pride and cream of the German navy. Dashing young officers did not relish stagnating in the home bound surface fleet. They rushed to serve in the daring, adventurous submarine arm. Admiral Holtzendorff anticipated combat - with American naval forces in due course.

Chancellor Bethmann-Holweg fought relentlessly for the Hague Conventions in submarine warfare. On 6 March 1916, the Kaiser publicly endorsed the chancellor's policy. They must not goad the United States into joining Britain in the war. Admiral Tirpitz protested bitterly. Submarines were 'sitting ducks' in surface warfare. Tirpitz could not condone that German U-boats must operate with their hands tied. The admiral demanded fully aggressive submarine operations. On 17 March 1916, the Kaiser overruled the navy's objections and Tirpitz resigned. Nevertheless, soon afterwards the naval high command ordered a U-boat attack on Sussex, a cross-channel steamer. Eighty Americans lost their lives.

President Wilson immediately sent an ultimatum without a time limit: unless the present methods of submarine warfare against passenger and freight carriers stopped, he would "sever relations with the German Empire altogether." Germany then promised: "To do its utmost to confine the operations of war, for the rest of its duration, to the fighting forces of the belligerents. No more merchant ships would be sunk without warning and without saving human lives." But on 4 May, another German note to the United States took a different tack. It warned that if all belligerents did not obey the Hague Convention, Germany must reserve complete liberty of decision.

Meanwhile, political intrigue in Mexico continued. Germany secretly sought to ally with Mexico. Submarine bases next to American shipping lanes could swing the sea war in Germany's favor. Any potential leader who might provide naval bases to German submarines received a promise of aid. A volatile political climate in Mexico would also keep American military assets busy.

Admiral Tirpitz had failed to move the politicians toward unrestricted U-boat operations. Admiral Scheer, after the High Seas Fleet's narrow escape at Jutland, had better success. Scheer convinced the Kaiser and the chancellor that the fleet could not compete on the high seas. Germany's heroic commerce raiding on the vast oceans had also faded away. The auxiliaries' total war effort fell short in strangling British commerce. Germany must use 'unrestricted' U-boat warfare to defeat Britain before the United States entered the war. On 9 January 1917, a secret message from the Kaiser went to all vessels of his navy: "order that unrestricted submarine warfare be launched with the greatest vigor, beginning on 1 February. You will immediately take the necessary steps."

In Washington on 31 January, when the hour for protest had passed, Count Johann-Heinrich von Bernstorff walked into the State Department. Grim-faced, he told Secretary of State Robert Lansing that the Kaiser had ordered the resumption of unrestricted submarine warfare. Lansing favored an immediate break with Germany but President Wilson dallied. Facing the cabinet, Wilson argued one way and then the other. Finally he agreed to break diplomatic relations with Germany. The president believed this would force Germany to recant.

President Wilson addressed Congress on 3 February 1917. He had broken diplomatic relations with Germany. Wilson still could not believe the Germans "meant to do in fact what they have warned us they feel at liberty to do." However, the president warned if German submarines sank American ships and caused American casualties he would take steps: "One more overt act and we'll be proud to fight."

Although Admiral Scheer appreciated the potential of submarine warfare, he lived by 'old-time' naval principles. Scheer and his peers believed in decisive sea battles fought between capital ships. On 31 January Admiral Scheer stressed his grand vision of a High Seas Fleet when he issued the Kaiser's 'unrestricted U-boat' orders to the fleet. Signaling from SMS *Kaiser Wilhelm II* that all naval units must subordinate themselves to the new submarine offensive, he stressed his long-term view: "A combat-ready High Seas Fleet ultimately bears the maritime prestige of a state. The peace we aim to force through with submarines, must become the renascence of the German High Seas Fleet."

Ominously, despite the off-and-on unrestricted tactics of the U-boats, Admiral Jellicoe had written in October 1916: "Allied and neutral losses to submarines are rising to alarming monthly totals". . . . "Unless something is done, we may be forced into peace terms not justified by the land situation."

At the end of February Germany's new policy showed instant effect. U-boats sank one-hundred-seventy-one allied ships plus sixty-six neutrals for 468,000 total tons. January's comparative figures numbered ninety-six allied and sixty-five neutral ships for 293,000 tons. Jellicoe's gloomy forecast seemed credible. Great Britain also faced a crucial cash crunch that required financial aid.

CHAPTER 5:

The Zimmermann Telegram.

In London, Winston Churchill's communications brainchild had expanded exponentially. Signals Intelligence (SIGINT) intercepted, decoded and processed messages from every source. The original group in Room 40 now formed the nucleus of a brilliant team of specialists. Captain Hall's department complemented intelligence activities with top-secret communications intercepts.

During 1915, good fortune gifted Hall with a new dimension to Room 40. Early in the year, an Austrian wireless engineer had helped the Germans repair a wrecked transmission station in Brussels. English-born Alexander Szek then worked for the Germans at the wireless station. When the station's new traffic first appeared, Room 40 could not read the codes. Hoping for repatriation to Britain, Szek copied some columns from a German diplomatic code book used at the station. He offered the list to a Belgian secret agent. Subsequently, British agents contacted Szek and persuaded him to copy the complete code book. Szek spent two months of furtive, painstaking copying. The Secret Service ultimately delivered the completed code to the British military attaché in The Hague. Major Laurie Oppenheim sent it to 'Blinker' Hall.

Consequently, without advising Admiral Ewing, Captain Hall founded a diplomatic annex to Room 40. Sir George Young headed this section with help from ex-Etonians Faudel-Phillips and Nigel de Grey - plus the Reverend William Montgomery. They set up the new unit to exploit captured German diplomatic codes. Captain Hall held tight personal control over the operation.

Additional good luck handed another important diplomatic code to Room 40. Wilhelm Wassmuss, a flamboyant German vice consul, had floundered into personal problems in Bushire, Persia. Wassmuss had strived to arouse Muslim Baktiari tribes into a 'jihad' against the British. In his travels, Herr Wassmuss visited the house of a local khan in Bebehan. This quasi friend betrayed him to the British garrison. As the troops approached to arrest him, Wassmuss fled frantically on horseback, leaving his luggage behind. Wassmuss's lost baggage eventually landed in the storage cellars of the India Office in London. Following 'Blinker' Hall's inspired hunch, a search of the luggage turned up Wassmuss's diplomatic codes.

Secretly peeking into Germany's diplomatic traffic proved difficult. Wireless carried some signals but telegraph cables processed most trans-Atlantic messages. When Germany's cable lines failed from British sabotage, their diplomats switched to the Swedish cable system. Strong British complaints ended this route in the summer of 1915. Germany then translated their diplomatic traffic into Swedish and cabled messages from Stockholm via Buenos Aires to Washington. This system also passed through England. In 1916, Hall's people identified and intercepted the German messages. Room 40 named this routing 'the Swedish roundabout.'

Since the beginning of the war President Wilson frequently exchanged notes with the Kaiser. Wilson yearned to mediate a peace treaty. At the end of 1916, Count Johann von Bernstorff suggested that speedier communications might aid the process. Wilson readily agreed to Germany using the American transatlantic cable, although this violated neutrality rules. Anyway, the American cable passed through Britain and Room 40 currently intercepted State Department ciphers. Secretly reading Wilson's coded messages, to and from Colonel House, the President's confidential agent, had offered a simple challenge. Blinker Hall's people now intercepted the German signals in the American diplomatic traffic.

Captain William Reginald Hall, a self-confident, arrogant officer, selected and distributed the diplomatic intercepts personally. Hall unilaterally decided that sharing the top-secret source carried an unacceptable risk. The DNI decided which information to share with other departments. Cabinet Secretary Maurice Hankey once discovered that Hall had kept 'priceless' intelligence from Lord Arthur Balfour, First Lord of the Admiralty.

In 1917, Hall had secret agents operating in the United States and South America. The local British naval attaché usually quarter-backed the flow of information. Captain Hall fully understood the anxieties that the United States president bore regarding Mexico. Anti-

Americanism in the southern neighbor had constantly aggravated Wilson. General Caranza, with American support, had overthrown President Huerta in July 1914. Germany helped transport the ousted ex-president to Barcelona, Spain where he continued to draw large support from international business interests. General Huerta returned secretly to New York on 13 April 1915: German agents had promised to support a coup against Caranza. 'Blinker' Hall had a special agent monitoring the meetings in the Manhattan Hotel, New York. Subsequently, various teams of agents 'unobtrusively' tailed Huerta from New York around the southern states. Finally, FBI agents arrested the Mexican ex-president in El Paso, Texas. Ultimately, General Huerta died of natural causes in prison - before achieving any insurrection.

Emilio Zapata and Pancho Villa, also caused headaches for Wilson. On 9 March 1916, Pancho Villa raided Columbus, New Mexico. Four hundred Mexican horsemen plundered the town and killed twenty Americans. President Wilson immediately sent General Pershing, with 6600 troops into Mexico in search of Villa. Simultaneously, Emilio Zapata had contemptuously chased President Caranza out of Mexico City. This volatile Mexican history proved a golden asset to Britain in 1917, when Room 40 intercepted a telegram that changed the course of the war.

Early in the morning of 17 January 1917, Nigel de Grey had finished night duty with Reverend Montgomery. Grey found Captain Hall in company with his personal assistant Claud Serocold: "Do you want to bring America into the war?" Grey asked Hall. "Yes, of course, my boy - Why?" Hall was instantly attentive. "I think I have something here for you." Grey handed him an incomplete interception. The telegram originated from Arthur Zimmermann, German foreign minister, sent to Ambassador Count Bernstorff in Washington:

' Berlin to Washington. W 158. 16 January 1917.
Most secret for Your Excellency's personal information and to be handed onto the Imperial Minister in (?) Mexico with. . . . by a safe route.

We propose to begin on the 1st. February unrestricted submarine warfare. In doing this however we shall endeavor to keep America neutral . . . (?) If we should not (? succeed in doing

so) we propose to (? Mexico) an alliance upon the following basis:
(joint)conduct of war
(joint) conclusion of peace.
. . . Your Excellency should for the present inform the
President secretly (? that we expect) war with the USA (possibly)
(. . . . Japan) and at the same time to negotiate between us and
Japan . . . .
Please tell the President that . . . . Our submarines . . . . Will
compel England to peace within a few months.
Acknowledge receipt. Zimmermann. '

Wide-open gaps riddled the message but it brought a jubilant gleam to Hall's eyes. 'Blinker' instantly realized the political potential of the telegram: Germany intended to open full scale unrestricted submarine warfare. If the United States declared war, Germany offered Mexico an alliance to attack the Americans. But a massive problem instantly arose. How could Hall warn the United States without exposing his clandestine interception group? SIGINT had found the telegram on 'the Swedish Roundabout' and the Americans' transatlantic cable. Hall could not reveal either source. Room 40's activities must remain top secret.

Hall recognized that British Foreign Secretary Arthur Balfour enjoyed great prestige in the United States. If Lord Balfour alerted the Americans they might accept his word without specific proof. At all costs, Hall must keep the existence and skill of his diplomatic code breakers unknown. 'Blinker' considered stealing a copy of the Swedish version in Buenos Aires. But how could he prove the telegram had ever reached Mexico? This was a quest that challenged the legendary intellect of the most successful DNI on record.

On 5 February - three weeks after the first interception - Hall met Permanent Undersecretary Lord Hardinge at the Foreign Office. He showed Hardinge the original decrypt - still with some gaps. Hall said that the British minister in Mexico, Edward Thurston, expected to get a copy of Bernstorff's ongoing telegram to Mexico City. 'Blinker' told Hardinge the German legation in Mexico would likely use a different code from the German traffic to Washington. Hall's people could possibly decode the entire Mexican version.

Thurston secretly obtained a copy of the 'Mexican edition' of the Zimmermann telegram on 10 February. The coding closely resembled the 'Wassmuss' code. Four weeks after the initial interception in London, 'Blinker' Hall had a complete text of Zimmermann's telegram - Mexican version. On 19 February Hall reviewed the exact script that would later appear in the American Press on 1 March 1917:

> **We intend to begin on the first of February unrestricted submarine warfare. We shall endeavor in spite of this to keep the USA neutral. In the event of this not succeeding we make Mexico a proposal of alliance on the following terms:**
>> **Make war together.**
>> **Make peace together.**
>> **Generous financial support and an undertaking on our part that Mexico is to reconquer the lost territory in Texas, New Mexico and Arizona. The settlement in detail is left to you.**
>> **You will inform the (Mexican) President of the above most secretly as soon as the outbreak of war with USA is certain, and add the suggestion, that he should on his own initiative, invite Japan to immediate adherence and at the same time mediate between Japan and ourselves.**
>> **Please call the President's attention to the fact that the ruthless employment of our submarines now offers the prospect of compelling England in a few months to make peace.**
>> **Zimmermann.**

Captain Hall, DNI, intended using Zimmermann's treacherous message to Britain's best advantage. Within hours Hall phoned Eddie Bell, the American diplomatic liaison with British Intelligence. Bell came immediately to Hall's room at the Admiralty and read the Zimmermann telegram - off the record. This 'completed' version showed a clear invitation to Mexico to reconquer Texas, New Mexico, and Arizona. Bell asked for an official copy but Hall told him it would have to come from the Foreign Office.

Next day Hall visited Ronald Campbell, Hardinge's private secretary. 'Blinker' suggested they simply give the telegram to Bell who would give it to Walter Page, the American ambassador - thence to the president. Or they could leak it to the American press without any indication that the British government had any part. Hardinge preferred to 'leak' the document. However he intimated that Foreign Secretary Lord Balfour had full confidence in Hall to 'correctly' handle the problem. Hall then met Eddie Bell and Dr. Walter Page in the American embassy. They resolved that Balfour would hand the decrypted message to Ambassador Page on Friday, 23 February - for the personal attention of President Wilson.

In Washington on 24 February, American Secretary of State Lansing was enjoying a short vacation. Acting Secretary Frank Polk received Page's telegram. The ambassador in London had warned earlier the importance of the incoming information. When Polk saw the content, he immediately sought a meeting with President Wilson. At 20:30 he walked briskly across the street to the White House and gave the president the Zimmermann brief. President Wilson calmly read the information. Was this a hoax? Where did they get this telegram? Wilson ordered Polk to get proof of the Zimmermann message.

The American president had vigorously demanded that the Kaiser cancel unrestricted submarine attacks. A huge backlog of wary merchant ships lay waiting in American ports. Wilson had consequently initiated a bill to arm American freighters. Senator Lodge had pressured Wilson to immediately declare war on Germany but the president insisted they remain neutral. Lodge wanted the war issue settled before Congress recessed on 4 March for nine months. His group threatened to filibuster and gain an extra session. Wilson gave his 'Armed Ship Bill' speech to Congress on Monday 26 February. He did not mention the Zimmermann conspiracy, believing it might influence the vote. Meanwhile Senators Stone and Hitchcock had turned against the president's bill. Wilson dug in his heels with typical tough mindedness. On Wednesday 28 February, he let Hitchcock read the Zimmermann telegram. The senator's furious reaction culminated in his agreement to lead the President's Armed Ships Bill through the House. Secretary Lansing also advised Hitchcock to apprize Senator Stone about the German-Mexican conspiracy.

Meanwhile, Lansing had searched the State Department cables and dug out a long coded signal addressed to Count Bernstorff, dated

17 January. Undersecretary Polk had also turned up a copy of Bernstorff's coded telegram to Mexico City. They wired this telegram to the American embassy in London with instructions to decode it. Later that evening Lansing received E.M. Hood of the Associated Press as a guest at his home. The AP executive agreed to publish the content of the Zimmermann telegram. Hood guaranteed the government's source would remain undefined. On 1 March, the New York *Times* led the American Press in headlining the news: ***Germany wishes to involve Mexico and Japan in the European war. Mexico might attack Texas, Arizona and New Mexico.*** Irrepressible American anger rolled across the country from New England to the Pacific Ocean. Wilson could no longer claim his people wanted neutrality. The European war had suddenly hammered on the door of every American.

Events tumbled rapidly into place. On 4 March, the senators' filibuster achieved its objective - an extra session would convene on 26 April. However, on 9 March Wilson used executive privilege to put the Armed Ship Bill into effect. At this time, Walter Page sent an urgent message from London: **"Failing US government loan, Britain cannot buy another gun or crate of goods from America."** Wilson made no move to reply.

Predictably, the publication of the Zimmermann telegram forced Wilson into his worst scenario - a declaration of war. Raging American public reaction knocked Wilson off his stubborn neutrality policy. On 16 March, another jab to the American psyche crumpled Wilson. U-boats torpedoed two American freighters - *City of Memphis* and *Illinois*. President Wilson called a special session of Congress. Following a tumultuous reception on the evening of 2 April, Wilson made his war speech to Congress. At 03:00 on 6 April 1917, after a vote 82:6 in the Senate, the House voted 373:50 to support the president. The United States declared war on Germany.

American entry into the war instantly strengthened Britain's war effort but she had little time left. Shipyard production could not match the losses to U-boats. Admiral Jellicoe coordinated with American Rear Admiral William S. Simms to cut the drastic shipping losses. Simms suggested a convoy defense against U-boats. Despite a huffy rebuff from the British Admiralty, Simms's strategy went into play. Prime Minister Lloyd George provided the necessary impetus. Beginning in

May 1917, the first convoy sailed from Gibraltar. Another, from Hampton Roads, Virginia soon followed. Both achieved outstanding success and the system became fundamental in naval strategy against submarine attack. Then a concentrated building program of antisubmarine vessels and detection methods raced to beat the threat of new U-boat production. Timely development of new weapons, like the depth charge, helped the allied effort.

Exposure of the Zimmermann conspiracy effectively sealed the Kaiser's fate. Massive American production, coupled with British antisubmarine 'know–how', soon swamped the U-boat offensive. 'Blinker' Hall had played his trump card perfectly. President Wilson had assured the Senate of the authenticity of the Zimmermann plot. Wilson claimed American agents had found and decoded the text. Truly, Britain's Nigel de Grey worked with Eddie Bell in the American embassy and covered this half-truth. They used Room 40 code books to decode Bernstorff's telegram to Mexico - the copy that Washington had sent to Walter Page. In addition, Captain Hall carefully protected Room 40's existence from German cognisance; he provided inconclusive evidence implicating Count von Bernstorff.

Shortly after the president severed relations with Germany, Bernstorff and his embassy staff embarked from New York on the *Frederick VIII*, a Danish ship. On 9 February the Danish vessel received assurance of safe passage across the Atlantic if she called into Halifax, Canada. Customs officials in Halifax began searching every corner of the vessel on 16 February. The Canadians rummaged for twelve days. They finally confiscated a sealed trunk from Bernstorff's luggage that held Swedish documents. Zimmermann had sent his telegram on the 'Swedish Roundabout' plus the American cable. 'Blinker' Hall then leaked untrue information that the seals on Bernstorff's trunk were found broken in New York. It appeared that somehow an American agent had discovered the original telegram.

In Germany, a frantic exchange of telegrams between Berlin and Mexico tried to pin down the break in security. The ambassador to Mexico, von Eckhard, proved himself and his secretary Magnus, free of error and blame. Von Eckhard pointed an accusing finger in the direction of Count von Bernstorff. On his end, Foreign Minister Zimmermann faced a fierce interrogation that led to a six-hour debate in the Reichstag. Zimmermann emerged with a vote of confidence - it was his responsibility to seek allies. Unfortunately, the details had prematurely leaked out. Arthur Zimmermann continued to use the 'Wassmuss' code when contacting von Eckhard in Mexico. Room 40 read the signals with relief. They showed that Zimmermann had not considered cable interception and decoding as a possible leak.

However, the State Department in Washington nervously expected Zimmermann to deny the publicized telegram. Penetrating Senate questions still hung in the air regarding its authenticity. Robert Lansing had promised to protect the involvement of British intelligence at any cost. Zimmermann's denial could make this very difficult. On 3 March, Ambassador Zimmermann gave a press conference in Berlin. In response to a question that begged his denial of the telegram, Zimmermann accepted full responsibility. He confirmed the Mexican offer as legitimate but they would begin negotiations only if America declared war on Germany. Zimmermann's self-admitted guilt sent a wave of relief through the State Department.

Meantime, in London, they knighted 'Blinker' Hall for his Zimmermann feat. Further, he knew that Zimmermann had sent another telegram to Mexico City on 5 March, telling von Eckard to begin negotiations with Mexico immediately. This telegram surfaced in Zimmermann's personal files in 1920. Captain Hall also knew the extent, if any, of British tampering that may have 'embroidered' the Mexican version of the Zimmermann telegram. Future Admiral Sir William Reginald 'Blinker' Hall and his Room 40 group of specialists 'carried on'.

CHAPTER 6:
Last Post for the Imperial Navy.

Seven million casualties spilled their lifeblood into the fields and trenches of Europe during the First World War. Four years of vicious conflict sapped the human energy of a generation. On 29 September 1918, the Allies finally smashed through the last German resistance on the Western Front. The Hindenburg Line collapsed along a ten-mile stretch. General Ludendorff, Chief of the Army General Staff, requested the civil authorities to arrange an armistice. Prince Max of Baden, the provisional Chancellor of Germany accepted the task of negotiating with the United States president. Paradoxically, Admiral Scheer had recently ordered the production of 450 new submarines. Scheer intended to expand the highly successful U-boat offensive but it was a ploy without meaning. Germany could not build this number of submarines. At best, it might help negotiate an acceptable armistice agreement.

Prince Max opened tentative proceedings with President Wilson on 3 October. Shortly afterwards - 16 October - the prince guaranteed the president an end to 'unrestricted' submarine warfare.

When peace negotiations began, the Naval High Command analyzed the High Seas Fleet's predicament. Admiral Scheer could not accept defeat without a last-ditch battle. He wished to risk men and ships in a final engagement. German naval honor and any hope of rebuilding the fleet after a settlement lay in the balance. In this mood the High Command issued orders intended to engage British and American capital warships based at Rosyth. Operations Order 19 - an all-or-nothing sea battle - would take place on 30 October. They believed this desperate effort would sow the seeds of a new high seas fleet in the future. Sadly, two somnolent years in home ports as a 'fleet in being' had drained the fighting spirit of the High Seas Fleet. Socialistic tendencies had seeped into the chain of command. Discipline had deteriorated in step with careless ship maintenance. Quasi-rebellious complaints against harsh working conditions had met with severe punishment. In September, the High Command had ordered courts-martial for sailors showing mutinous behavior. Neither ships nor men could rally for active engagement. Fleet crews viewed Operations Order 19 as a futile 'death ride' against the enemy. Most of the sailors ignored Admiral Scheer's attempt to save face and naval honor. Some officers and a few ratings answered the call but a general mutiny broke out to obstruct the order. Shortly afterwards - 4 November - mutinous sailors seized Kiel in violent demonstrations.

Fortunately for Scheer's pride and the Kaiser's fleet they did not sail out. British intelligence in room 40 had warned the Admiralty of the German fleet's preparations. Admiral Sir David Beatty would have relished surprising and annihilating the overmatched Germans with his Grand Fleet. During the war Beatty had come close to destroying Admiral von Hipper's elite Battle Cruiser Squadron. The British admiral's squadron had advantage in size, speed and fire power against Hipper. However, good luck and good seamanship had allowed the German admiral to endure with most of his units afloat. Beatty had dreamed of permanently ending Germany's naval expansion. He envisioned a full-scale engagement of both fleets that would result in a spectacular British victory. Admiral Beatty wanted to smash the German fleet beyond any chance of rebuilding. As C-in-C Grand Fleet on 21 October 1918, Beatty sent a memo to the British War Cabinet:

> *"Ref: The Naval Terms of an Armistice: To achieve the destruction of German sea power and reduce Germany to the status of a second rate naval power it is necessary to lay down, in the terms of the Armistice, conditions which could be commensurate with the results of a naval action. Remove the power of the High Seas Fleet now, and . . . . reduce the continental nation of Germany to that of a second rate naval power corresponding to her geographical position and requirements, and our position at sea is at once secured. Great Britain in the future will be spared a race with Germany for sea supremacy."*

In September, as General Ludendorff's army buckled under unrelenting pressure, a group of senior officers met in Spa, Belgium. They discussed terms and conditions that might flow from a peace accord with the Entente. General von Gündell headed the commission with Rear Admiral Meurer leading the navy contingent and Baron von Lersner representing the foreign office. Junior Captain Erich Raeder attended the meetings while his ship - *Köln* - underwent repairs in dry dock. At the end of the conference Admiral Scheer hosted a dinner with special invitations to Field Marshal von Hindenburg and General Ludendorff. Over the past five years, Captain Raeder had served alongside Admiral Hipper in the Battle Cruiser Scouting Group. Hipper had supreme trust in his chief of staff. At the Spa naval meetings, Raeder worked with many important military and political figures. He contributed sensibly to the discussion and made a lasting impression on the senior officers.

Raeder returned to Wilhelmshaven and reported his findings to Admiral Hipper on 10 October. Germany's military and political situation was precarious. It seemed an armistice negotiation and peace settlement would result in a greatly diminished navy. All monarchial power representing both the Kaiser and the crown prince would be forced out of Germany. A few days later a major influenza epidemic struck *Köln*'s crew. Captain Raeder received orders to report to Berlin. As Chief of the Central Department of the *Reichsmarineamt* (RMA) he observed the dismantling of the nation and the navy at first hand. Germany's military and political systems imploded in tandem with ongoing armistice negotiations. The sailors' mutiny had grown into a minor rebellion and quickly reached inland to Berlin. Fearing internal spies, Admiral Scheer sent Raeder to Wilhelmshaven with a personal message to Admiral Hipper. Scheer promised that 'reliable troops' would arrive to ensure law and order. In Wilhelmshaven, Raeder rated the situation already out of control. His train journey back to Berlin took two days. Loyal troops constantly stopped and searched the train for rebels.

On 9 November 1918, Chancellor Prince Max of Baden announced the abdication of the Kaiser. President Wilson had refused to discuss peace terms that included any form of the monarchy. Prince Max then stepped aside in favor of Friedrich Ebert, the leader of the Social Democratic Party. Provisional Chancellor Ebert desperately needed the support of the army to maintain his temporary government. Fortunately, the army officers' corps had also decided that Ebert's Social Democrats could best serve Germany's immediate future. In the evening 9 November, Lt. General William Groener, who had replaced General

Ludendorff as Quartermaster General of the army, phoned Ebert from Spa. In his phone call Groener committed the army's support if Ebert promised to combat Bolshevism and maintain law and order. Chancellor Ebert readily agreed.

On 11 November 1918, Germany reluctantly signed the armistice agreement. German negotiators had expected armistice terms to fall near President Wilson's fourteen-point suggestions. But the harsh conditions finally imposed extended far beyond Wilson's well-publicized criteria. Vengeful allies wanted their pound of flesh, including mandatory internment of the German fleet. Surrendering their ships without a fight stirred resentful humiliation within the naval officers' corps. Only volunteers with special pay rates manned the warships on this dismal duty. The Imperial Navy's honor fell in tatters.

On 15 November 1918, the cruiser *Königsberg* sailed into the Firth of Forth carrying Rear Admiral Hugo Meurer. HMS *Cardiff* escorted her through thick fog to the Inchkieth light. While the German warship anchored, the destroyer HMS *Oak* kept vigil. It was early afternoon. After a four-hour delay *Königsberg* lowered a steam barge that flew a white flag atop the admiral's ensign. Rear Admiral Meurer's small party then crossed to the destroyer. A rapid 12-mile trip upstream ended in a transfer to HMS *Queen Elizabeth* where Admiral Sir David Beatty waited in his flagship's wardroom. The British admiral savored the total humiliation of the German officers. How could they give up everything without a fight?

Rear Admiral Hubert G. Brand and Captain Ernie Chatfield greeted the Germans at the rails of the flagship. Resplendent in full dress uniforms they briskly escorted Meurer's small party into the admiral's presence. Beatty sat regally at the massive mahogany dining table. Vice Admiral Sir Charles Madden and Rear Admiral Sir Osmond de B.Brock sat on each side of the admiral. A full-length painting of Lord Nelson gazed scornfully down on the Germans from the bulkhead behind the British officers. Without preamble Beatty stonily asked for Meurer's credentials and gave him a list of instructions. The list fell short of the complete surrender that Beatty and First Sea Lord Admiral Sir Rosslyn Wemyss had proposed. Many British politicians had refused to comply with Beatty's draconian demands. They feared the Germans might withdraw their armistice request or the Americans might conclude a separate agreement. Nevertheless, internment of the bulk of the High Seas Fleet inflicted horrific trauma on the German officers

Rear Admiral Meurer bore his pain with dignity. Meurer explained that mutiny had crippled the High Seas Fleet's fighting spirit. He stated that three plenipotentiaries from the Sailors' and Workers' Soviet now waited on board *Königsberg*. They had authorization to attend all conferences. Beatty responded with a sour expletive and refused to see them. After a short belligerent discussion, Beatty dismissed Meurer. He must return to his ship and study the conditions on the list. Next day, with tentative pen, Rear Admiral Meurer signed the documents: the Germans must deliver the major part of the High Seas Fleet into neutral ports for internment.

On 21 November, the downtrodden German navy steamed into Scottish waters. HMS *Cardiff* met the inbound warships at sea. The disgraced fleet slowly slipped past a congress of 370 British and allied warships. Germany's nine battleships, five battle cruisers, seven cruisers and forty-nine modern destroyers made an impressive if forlorn spectacle. Assuming the van position, *Cardiff* led the trailing line of ships into the Firth of Forth. The Grand Fleet waited in two majestic columns with the United States Sixth Battle Squadron in company. Shoals of numerable destroyers supported the big ships. Clearing May Island, *Cardiff* led the Germans between two parallel lines of oncoming dreadnought battleships. On a signal the giant battleships reversed course - turning 180 degrees with exquisite precision. Taking station on either side of the German ships they herded them like wayward sheep into their anchorage off Aberlady Bay. It was a crushing exhibition of contempt. In Beatty's mind the German navy had surrendered without a fight to the royal navy. Many of his contemporaries had a more magnanimous attitude toward the former foe. German sailors and ships had fought with admirable courage and valor during the few occasions when they had engaged the royal navy.

Lt-Commander H.H. Harwood, torpedo officer on board HMS *Royal Sovereign,* wrote a personal letter to an uncle on 27 November 1918, that described the scene. [Lt Cmdr. Harwood was destined to find fame in the Second World War when defeating the *Graf Spee* in the Battle of the River Plate.]

"... It really was a most extraordinary proceeding. We went alongside in our picket boat and were piped over the side in the usual manner. We were received by several of their officers. Their men were all aft smoking and lounging on the Quarter Deck. They have on board what they call ' Members of the Soldiers' and Workmen's Council'. They wear white and red armbands on their arms. The officers have to get all their orders signed by the Council but once they are signed, the officers have full power to carry them out. On the whole, there is quite a lot of discipline but the men seem to spend all their time smoking on the Quarter Deck. Needless to say, we were very formal. Grave salutes and no shaking of hands etc. - only strictly business remarks were passed. We were treated quite courteously, especially by the men. It is very hard to understand but I can't help thinking that the sailors think they are on our side against their officers. For instance, the men were much more inclined to show us details of their ship than were the officers. The ship - SMS Krönprinz Wilhelm (Little Willie) - was filthy and can't have been painted for years. ... I heard in one case the Captain and Executive officer of a German warship had both burst into tears - I am not surprised ... We left Rosyth yesterday [26 November] at noon with four Germans astern of us, SMS Bayern, Markgraf, Krönprinz Wilhelm, and König Albert with the remainder of our division astern of them. We arrived at Scapa Flow at 09:00 this morning after an uneventful trip. Our naviga-tor at once went on board and took them to their internment billets."*

Various royal navy units repeated this procedure until they securely interned all the German warships in Scapa Flow, Scotland. German Rear Admiral von Reuter held responsibility for the ships' behavior, with his Chief of Staff Lt-Commander Oldekop.

As time moved on, Lt-Cmdr Quaet-Faslem, commander of the dispatch boat that serviced the interned fleet, relayed a verbal instruc-tion to Oldekop: Germany must prevent the sharing of these warships amongst the victors. Thus, while the delegates in Versailles sought a final agreement, Reuter and his officers planned to scuttle the fleet. Finally, on 19 June 1919, the delegates hammered the Versailles Treaty into shape. Next day, Rear Admiral von Reuter read the naval terms in a special edition of the *Times*. Tears welled up in his eyes. Germany must surren-der all interned warships and demilitarize Heligoland. The treaty restricted the future numerical strength of the postwar German fleet in ships and personnel. Failure to accept the provisions of the treaty would result in the allies revoking the armistice and renewing the war. Von Reuter knew exactly how his navy must react. Months of contingency planning would deny the victors their spoils. Complying with a British order to reduce crew numbers, von Reuter had already sent most of the 'unreliable' sailors home. Paragraph 11 - a desperate attempt to save face - would commence at the first opportunity.

Incredibly, next day - 21 June - the Germans' jailor at Scapa Flow opened the door. Sir Sydney Fremantle sailed out his First Battle Squadron on torpedo exercises. As Fremantle's ships disappeared into the morning mist a signal ran up on *Emden's* foremast: *'Paragraph 11 - Acknowledge.'* Repeater flags, semaphore flashes, lamp signals and word of mouth instantly spread the coded order from ship to ship. Designated officers rushed below to open the sea-cocks. Simultaneously, petty officers mustered the crews and prepared to abandon ship. Eagerly, the chill Scottish waters roared into the doomed warships. Great vessels sinking and capsizing turned the Scapa Flow waters around Cava into a nightmarish scenario. SMS *Friedrich der Grosse*, a 24,380 ton flagship led the way. She rolled over amidst a thunderous roar of displaced air and sank to her grave. The last warship to disappear was SMS *Hindenburg* - a new 26,180 ton battle cruiser. At day's end, fifty still and silent warships lay settled on the bottom. Although the British beached some ships, the German High Command hailed the suicide of the fleet as a political success.

CHAPTER 7:
Resurrection: Admiral von Trotha and the Kapp Putsch.

Armistice discussions that formed the Versailles Peace Treaty ran from 11 November 1918 until 21 June 1919. It was a bitter seven month period of demands and counter demands. President Wilson's well-intentioned 14-point suggestions had vanished into the savage maw of national interests. During this time, Germany's provisional government tackled the daunting task of replacing a former autocratic system with a democratic republic. Free elections on 19 January 1919 saw six main parties competing for power. Provisional Chancellor Ebert's Social Democrats won the election. They convened a constituent assembly in Weimar on 6 February. The assembly then produced a new constitution - after forty sessions. A majority vote in the *Reichstag* legalized the new constitution on 31 July 1919.

Meanwhile, the naval officers' corps had experienced a seismic change in circumstances. Socialism had invaded the naval service at all levels and plunged the fleet officers into unacceptable conditions. Mutiny simmered just below the surface in the ports until it burst wide open. At the end of the war a half-flotilla of minesweepers lay at the dock in Bremerhaven. First Lieutenant Hans Langsdorff commanded the ships. Hunger and war fatigue had demoralized the crews. An armed group of rebels held the dock and demanded Langsdorff's surrender. They claimed to represent soldiers' councils, yet promised law and order. Langsdorff had fought at Jutland and proudly wore the Iron Cross. Later, he served on minesweepers and survived exposure in the North Sea when his ship hit a mine. Langsdorff had loyalty and courage to spare. When he wrote a letter to his mother on 14 November 1918, he explained his dilemma: "There will be slaughter if we try to get out of the trap. My honor codes tell me to fight until the last man against the enemy. However, I cannot permit my loyal men to die fighting Germans. Yet, I cannot endure my flag flying over revolutionaries. So I ordered the flag and pennants brought down." With great patience and sadness Langsdorff negotiated a peaceful surrender

As the war phased out, submarine and torpedo-boat crews maintained regular naval discipline. In contrast, the surface fleet had established Deck Officers' Associations and Sailors' Councils. They held strong representation in Wilhelmshaven, Kiel and Hamburg. In Berlin a Supreme Naval Council - the Council of 53 - aggressively pushed naval issues that the Congress of Workers and Soldiers raised. The Council of 53, a 'socialist parliament' of the navy, wished to independently regulate all naval matters. This included vetting every order issued from the naval command. The *Reichsmarineamt* (RMA) could not accept the upheavals in the navy. Admiral von Mann (Head of RMA) and Erich Raeder (Chief of the Central Department) dog-paddled in a socialist flood tide. This threatened to swamp their resolve to resurrect the old style navy. Fortunately, Chancellor Ebert's provisional government supported von Mann - for different reasons. Ebert feared a potential threat to his law and order program from a socialist navy. Von Mann complained that the Council of 53 continually obstructed the RMA's function and Ebert took action. The chancellor agreed to delay the passage of any resolutions proposed by the Council of 53 or the Congress of Workers' and Soldiers' Councils. Still, Admiral von Mann resigned - suffering ill-health. The government then found serious problems filling von Mann's position due to the agitation of the Council. How could an acting State Secretary of the Navy function as an 'errand boy' of the Council of 53? This rudderless situation at the RMA helped augment Erich Raeder's influence.

After the January elections, the RMA merged with the Admiralty Staff and Naval Cabinet into the Admiralty Office. The new Ebert government appointed Admiral Rogge acting State Secretary of the Naval Office - until they could select a permanent C-in-C Navy. They also appointed Gustav Noske as the People's Commissioner for Defense. An ardent socialist, Noske had served von Mann as an assistant in the RMA. When first elected in 1906, the former master butcher had brought strong trade union tendencies to the Reichstag. A physically powerful man, Noske held unbending loyalty to the nation. Possessed of a military mind, he naturally became expert in military matters. Noske swiftly took action to declaw the Council of 53. In early February he cut living allowances for the Council, allowing for only six representatives. Imperceptibly, the Council Movement lost support throughout Germany.

Captain Erich Raeder, Chief of the Central Office, strived to rebuild and reform the Naval Officers' Corps. Raeder seized every chance to fill the role of spokesman for the naval officers. He developed credibility and gained personal access to many important leaders in Berlin. Raeder's foremost agenda - rebuilding the navy - drove his every action. The Kaiser and Grand Admiral Tirpitz had perceived and planned a powerful High Seas Fleet. The dream had vanished with the loss of the war. Prince Heinrich of Prussia had declared it 'a sacred duty' to revive the fleet in the new Germany. Erich Raeder poured his full energies into the resurrection of the High Seas Fleet. He persistently steered the officers' corps on this course, through the trials and reversals ahead.

When President Ebert began screening candidates for chief of the navy, Raeder strongly advocated Admiral von Trotha. Raeder believed the acting chief, Admiral Rogge, fell short because he had never commanded a wartime force at sea. During the war a semi-feud had developed between the supporters of Tirpitz's practical war aims and the politicians' cautious policy. The Kaiser had dithered in uncertainty. Fortunately, von Trotha enjoyed the respect of Tirpitz and the exiled Kaiser. The popular admiral could conceivably draw support from both camps - a significant benefit. Astutely, Raeder approached Admiral Rogge for permission to speak to Commissioner Noske concerning Trotha's merits. Noske agreed with Raeder's assessment and suggested he should discuss the matter personally with President Ebert.

At a meeting on 11 January, Raeder learned that Noske had already approached Ebert. Using Raeder's points of argument, Noske had proposed Trotha. President Ebert agreed with Trotha's suitability. However, his government held doubts that the unruly sailors would accept Trotha. The admiral seemed too closely aligned with the Imperial High Seas Fleet.

On 13 January Kurt Baake, Chief of the *Reichskanzlei* (chancery), invited Admiral von Trotha to a special conference with Ebert. The government needed to probe Trotha's views on the current condition of the fleet. They wanted the admiral's ideas on the best way ahead in rebuilding the navy. Baake had earlier sounded out Trotha's feelings toward Germany's collapse and his willingness to serve the new government. Trotha passionately declared his commitment to the past but professed an unshakable belief in Germany's future. He advocated a powerful high seas fleet. Later, in company with Admiral Rogge, President Ebert assured Trotha the government would choose him as chief of the navy. Admiral von Trotha warned about the problem of reasserting the officers' authority while the Council of 53 existed. They all feared that drastic action against the Council might incite new revolts. Postponing Trotha's official appointment seemed prudent until they tamed the council movement and formed a new government. Ebert accordingly instructed his cabinet colleagues to avoid raising Trotha's appointment. He wished to forestall any protests from sailors distrustful of the officers' corps. Ultimately, on 26 March they officially appointed Admiral von Trotha as Chief of the Admiralty. The admiral held a seat in the new government's cabinet but did not have voting privileges.

Admiral von Trotha energetically pounced on his top priority. They must cleanse the navy of socialist influences. A superb fighting machine had turned into a rebellious rabble. Trotha assured all worthy officers they could depend on a secure future if they stayed in the service. Demobilization would retire undesirable elements. In the new *Reichsmarine* a small central core of loyal officers could expect future expansion. Von Trotha would resurrect the German navy.

In the National Assembly, a series of debates ended with passage of a Provisional Navy Bill on 16 April 1919. Sailors' Councils would revert to a system of elected representatives among the enlisted men. These electees could negotiate issues regarding pay, food, clothing, quarters and furloughs, through the chain of command. However, the bill excluded them from purely military matters. Defense Minister Noske clearly understood the necessity of military discipline - he firmly rejected the 'supreme navy council'. Nonetheless, the debates had revealed a serious distrust of the navy's loyalty to the republican government.

Meanwhile, angry submarine and torpedo boat officers and crews arrived home to a defeated nation. They felt driven to prove their national loyalty and fervor. Defense Minister Noske encouraged them to form volunteer naval brigades to help the government maintain law and order. The government gave them the brief to restrain aggressive social- ist and communist rebels. Two Naval *Freikorps* commanders quickly built formidable fighting units that gained both fame and infamy in their actions. The Ehrhardt Second Naval Brigade and the Lowenfeld Third Naval Brigade saw brief but violent action in 1919 and 1920. Lowenfeld commanded a 3500-man brigade of well-disciplined officers and men. During the spring and summer of 1919 they fulfilled assignments in Berlin and Silesia. In November, a battalion of Lowenfeld's troops helped government troops maintain law and order in Kiel. The commander claimed he rotated his men every eight weeks to avoid 'political contamination'. Fiercely nationalistic, Lowenfeld could not readily accept the alien republican system taking shape in Berlin. The Ehrhardt Brigade formed in Wilhelmshaven under the nominal control of the naval station. It grew to over four thousand men. They earned the reputation as 'the strongest and most battle-tested unit in the *Reichswehr*'. Ehrhardt's troops saw action in Berlin, Munich and Silesia. In late 1919 he stationed them in Doberitz, near Berlin. Also intensely nationalistic, the Ehrhardt Brigade supported a right-wing *Putsch* against the republican government in March 1920. Many senior naval officers saw the Naval *Freikorps* as a two-edged sword. Admiral Kussel, commander of the Kiel Naval Station, feared some of his best officers would be drawn into Lowenfeld's brigade. Kussel desperately needed these officers to purify and remold his own ranks. Other critics of the Naval *Freikorps* units forecast difficulties in returning them to sea-based roles after land-based action.

Meanwhile in Weimar, armistice discussions dragged on and preposterous peace terms leaked from the meetings: Germany was to take the blame for starting the war and pay horrendous reparations. Seizure of German industrial lands and overseas colonies would help pay the allies their costs of the war. Germany would only have a small naval force to protect the Baltic and North Atlantic seaboards. War criminals, including the Kaiser, must face trial.

The politicians vacillated between proposals and counter proposals while the military considered the option of refusal. On 5 June 1919, Admiral von Trotha strongly advised the government against signing the treaty. He objected to handing over top army and naval officers as war criminals. Trotha mustered a meeting on 19 June with General Reinhardt and Defense Minister Noske. Thirty senior officers attended this meeting to assess armed resistance to accepting the treaty. To date, the German government had received scant recognition of their counter proposals to the treaty terms. On 20 June Chancellor Scheidemann resigned in protest. President Ebert persuaded a fellow SPD member -

Gustav Bauer - to form a new government and the Center Party promised support. Matthias Erzberger then led the discussion to accept the treaty - with major qualifications. However, all anti-treaty discussion collapsed on 21 June when von Reuter scuttled the fleet at Scapa Flow. The allies immediately demanded that the German government accept the treaty or face a relapse into war. President Ebert contacted General Groener to check the military situation. Groener advised that neither he nor the field marshals could support any renewed war.

On 22 June 1919, the Reichstag voted 237:138 to accept the Treaty of Versailles as dictated. But on 24 June, Admiral von Trotha officially refused to recognize the treaty - even with the noted qualifications. Trotha organized the naval officers' corps to support his refusal and threatened to resign in protest. Chancellor Bauer persuaded the admiral to remain and Defense Minister Noske fully agreed. Consequently, Trotha had effectively separated the navy from the government's stated policy.

Meanwhile, day-to-day violence continued throughout Germany. Early in 1920 communist-led strikers attacked the naval arsenal at Kiel. They seized the dockyard and arrested Admiral von Levetzow and four hundred officers. One of these officers, First Lieutenant Karl Dönitz, lost his command of a 'loyal' torpedo boat. Dönitz had served since January 1917 on U-boats and earned the Iron Cross. In September 1918, while commanding UB-68, he lost his boat in action. Taken as a prisoner of war, he was repatriated in 1919. At Kiel, the government reestablished order and reinstated Dönitz as an officer in the *Reichsmarine*. Later, he received command of Torpedo Boat T-157.

Admiral von Trotha's vision of the new navy took a definite form. The German navy must represent devoted unselfish service to the national interest. Governments may change but the navy must remain constant. Prior fealty to the Kaiser must devolve to absolute loyalty to the national government. Trotha worked tirelessly to convince the best naval officers to stay in the service. Gradually a semblance of order took hold in the officers' corps as he carefully weeded out socialism. Throughout this period, Erich Raeder remained a close and trusted advisor to the admiral.

Increasingly, fallout from the Versailles Treaty created a hard core of nationalists. Many people disagreed with the republican government's policies. When the allies gave the government a list of war criminals on 3 February 1920, it included many senior naval officers. They listed Tirpitz, Scheer, Behncke, Ingenohl, Trotha and Raeder along with twenty-nine U-boat captains. On 6 February, a group of these officers gave notice they would not submit to the jurisdiction of a foreign court. Von Trotha's name on the list brought a fierce rallying cry from the navy. An angry telegram to Defense Minister Noske from Admiral von Levetzow expressed the navy's total loyalty to Trotha - come what may. Noske assured von Levetzow that the government did not intend to surrender Trotha or any other officers. Still, a groundswell of anti-government sentiment percolated in the navy and army officers' corps. Finally, it exploded in a violent right wing *putsch* that overthrew the government. In March 1920, Wolfgang Kapp with the military support of Ehrhardt's Brigade seized Berlin. Kapp had found political encouragement from Ludendorff's circle and many high profile naval officers. However, a general strike closed down the nation and thwarted Kapp's coup. The government accused Admiral von Trotha of complicity in the *putsch* and demanded Gustav Noske's resignation. They arrested 171 naval officers who had supported Kapp and discharged or prematurely retired them from the navy.

When the chaos settled, the new defense minister, Otto Gessler, recalled Vice Admiral Paul Behncke from retirement and made him chief of naval staff. Then Gessler appointed Rear Admiral Zenker as Flag Officer, North Sea. Captain Erich Raeder came under scrutiny because of his close ties to Admiral Trotha. Although exonerated, he assumed a minor position in the Archives Section. Taking advantage of this change in fortunes, Raeder studied the intricacies of cruiser warfare. Captain Raeder later published two historical volumes concerning cruisers. In addition, he attended courses at the University of Berlin studying political science, administrative law and economics.

Admiral Erich Raeder

First Lord Winston Churchill & First Sea Lord Fisher.

– DiegoLascano

Rear Admiral Sir Christopher Cradock   – Diego Lascano

SMS Dresden
– Diego Lascano

SMS Dresden
trapped in Chile

Admiral Maximilian Graf von Spee – Diego Lascano

Sub-Lieut Heinrich and Sub-Lieut Otto von Spee

Tonnen: 11 600
Länge: 143,8 m
Breite: 21,6 m
Besatzung: 764

S. M. Panzer-Kreuzer „Scharnhorst"

SMS Scharnhorst

–Diego Lascano

Rear Admiral Sir Frederick Doveton Sturdee — Diego Lascano

Grand Admiral Alfred von Tirpitz

– DIEGO LASCANO

William II, the Kaiser, King of Prussia   – DIEGO LASCANO

*From top: SMS Krönprinz Wilhelm (Scapa Flow), SMS König and SMS
Markgraf* —Tait Archives

CHAPTER 8:
Admiral Raeder: C-in-C Reichsmarine.

Following the Kapp *Putsch,* Admirals Behncke and Zenker teamed with Defense Minister Otto Gessler to mend the navy's bedraggled image. Primarily, they strived to assure the government of navy loyalty to the republic. But the government kept a jaundiced eye on the military and the navy in particular. Ultimately, by 1922 relative law and order prevailed. The admirals realistically assessed the prospects of the navy within the Versailles Treaty. Two small fleets, one for the North Sea and the other for the Baltic, were in place. Each fleet had one ancient battleship, two old cruisers and eleven destroyers. Now, the treaty allowed some replacement warships. Admiral Behncke had decided to concentrate on new cruisers and destroyers. They laid down the light cruiser *Emden* in December 1921 and received a budget for three more to follow. As *Emden* neared completion in 1924, they laid down *Möwe* - their first new destroyer. Admiral Behncke had steered the navy through terrible political seas and restored a reasonable balance. Rebuilding the fleet could go ahead with caution.

In 1923 Behncke had asked his designers for battleship plans that would satisfy the treaty and lead to the renewal of the surface fleet. But replacing obsolete battleships caused a serious clash between the government and the navy. Popular opinion decried spending massive funds on battleships when the people needed food. If the military budget could afford such expense, they preferred army equipment to battleships. Conversely, naval high command firmly believed the growth of the nation and the *Reichsmarine* depended on building a new *Panzerschiff.*

Admiral Zenker replaced Admiral Behncke as C-in-C *Reichsmarine* in 1924. Zenker picked up the baton and ran with renewed energy in the same direction as Behncke. The design department produced two battleship plans that Zenker rejected. Then he chose the third design - *Deutschland* Class - as the best compromise for a new capital ship. This warship carried six 11-inch guns, had 26-knot speed and prototype diesel engines to give immense range. They concentrated these formidable qualities into approximately 10,000 tons to satisfy the treaty. Welded hulls and wide use of aluminum saved enough weight to permit the huge armament. In 1927, amid a storm of protest, the *Reichstag* voted funding to build one replacement battleship. A referendum in March 1928, gave the navy a fractional green light (255:203) to build the new battleship. Still, ongoing controversy delayed construction until after the election in May 1928.

During the referendum campaign a military financial scandal crashed into the news. Otto Gessler, the defense minister admitted he had diverted military funds to illegal uses. A secret fund had purchased illicit arms from Italy. It had also financed submarine and aircraft development - contrary to the treaty. This scandal revealed the military contempt for the treaty and the government. Although personal corruption did not surface, the Lohmann Affair toppled Admiral Zenker and Otto Gessler from their posts. Zenker tried half-heartedly to defend the expenditures but resigned with the defense minister when facing a furious *Reichstag*.

Meanwhile Captain Erich Raeder had rapidly advanced from his post in the Archives Section of the Admiralty. In July 1922 he reached rear admiral rank and moved to Inspector of Training - an important and prestigious post. Two years later - July 1924 - Raeder took command of light forces in the North Sea. Then in October they promoted him to vice admiral and made him C-in-C Baltic Fleet. Previously, in 1920 Raeder had given solid advice to Admiral Levetzow, then chief of the naval station at Kiel. Raeder suggested that Levetzow's civilian friends should defend the admiral against government charges of disloyalty. As C-in-C Baltic in 1924, Raeder followed his own advice and aggressively courted the civilian leaders in Kiel. The vice admiral wished to make himself and the navy acceptable to the public. Following his appointment to the Naval War College, Raeder developed close ties to the university community in Kiel. Nonetheless, in 1926 a prominent Kiel politician, *Reichstag* Deputy Eggerstedt, scathingly attacked Raeder for alleged association with right-wing anti-government groups. Raeder promptly sent a letter to prominent Kiel citizens denying the charges. He assured them that all ties to such groups were forbidden under his mandate.

The Lohmann Affair had buried the naval career of C-in-C Admiral Zenker. Raeder's name surfaced as a possible replacement and triggered a fierce public outcry. Deputy Eggerstedt bemoaned the idea that Raeder should lead the *Reichsmarine*. He accused him of throttling liberal tendencies in the Baltic Fleet. "Replacing Zenker, 'the red admiral', with Raeder," he argued, "would set back the republican direction of the military."

Admiral Levetzow took up the cudgel to support his friend Raeder. The retired admiral identified three possible competitors for the highest post in the *Reichsmarine*. Then he asked Raeder for his opinion on them - Admirals Bauer, Oldekopf and Mommsen. Raeder reasoned that Admiral Bauer (Class of 1892) had seniority; Mommsen (Class of 1891) had retired; Oldekopf (Class of 1895) was too young and inexperienced. Raeder thought that Admiral Bauer would probably have Zenker's support. Levetzow then wrote a letter to Graf Friedrich von der Schulenberg, praising Raeder's qualifications. He emphasized that Raeder would bring 'old schooling' to the navy. Graf von Schulenberg was a powerful member of the German National People's Party (DNVP). Admiral von Tirpitz held court as a 'grey eminence' in this party. Von Schulenberg assured Levetzow that the new defense minister, General Groener, would seriously consider Raeder's appointment. The count believed that Groener would choose the best man, despite seniority.

General Groener consulted General Kurt von Schleicher, a powerful leader in the defense ministry (WA), to check Raeder's suitability. Von Schleicher, a wily politician, suggested that Groener should make the changeover from Zenker to Raeder 'quietly'. However, the social democratic wire service broke the story and publicly announced Raeder's candidacy. A storm of objection immediately greeted the news. Angry critics recalled Raeder's ties to the imperial royal family. Then followed accusations of an association with the *Wiking Union*, a right-wing group. They also mentioned his questionable military attitude toward the republic. Front line Berlin newspapers howled with alarm. *Morgenpost* headlines asked: *"Imperial Admiral - Chief of Republican Navy?"* *Tageblatt* went further: *"Raeder was 'Spiritus Rector' in Admiralty support of the Kapp Putsch."* *Rote Fahn*e simply labeled Raeder as a Fascist. On the Conservative side, *Neue Preussische Zeitung* satisfied itself with criticism of Defense Minister Groener's leaning toward the left. They pointed to

Groener's inability to oppose 'Republican arrogance'. His edict to force active naval officers to resign from the Imperial Yacht Club brought fears of 'further encroachment'. Chancellor Hermann Müller kept a close eye on the press reports.

Dr. Hermann Punder the undersecretary of state, wrote to Groener on 22 September: *"The Chancellor does not wish any involvement in the selection of a C-in-C Reichsmarine but it could cause problems in the cabinet if charges against Raeder are true."* Paradoxically, Dr. Punder advised Müller that Raeder was a 'sensible and moderate man'. The state secretary, Dr. Otto Meissener, also vouched for Raeder. Still, the chancellor insisted on Groener's written opinion. Consequently, the defense minister requested Captain Friedrich Gotting, naval representative in the WA, to prepare a full report. Groener required an examination of all charges against Reader. Captain Gotting circulated a transcript of a Raeder speech, presented on 22 March 1928 to a civilian group in Kiel. Notably, General Schleicher received a copy. This speech formed the basis for Gotting's report to Groener. Admiral Raeder then successfully answered all questions from Gotting and Defense Minister Groener.

On 25 September, although battered with controversy, Admiral Raeder felt confident of Groener's support. In a typical act of reverse psychology he phoned Captain Gotting. Raeder offered to resign if Groener could not support his candidacy 100 percent. This would forestall any further embarrassment for the navy. Raeder also insisted on a complete clarification of specific charges alleged against his person.

Captain Gotting assured Raeder that Groener had found 'little truth' in the press attacks. The defense minister would not change his mind about Raeder's appointment. Meanwhile, a few isolated press reports carried some support for the harassed admiral. On 30 September, the *Frankfurter Zeitung* published a letter from Dr. Baumgarten, a professor of theology at Kiel. Dr. Baumgarten, a well known and respected Republican, attested to Raeder's unquestioned loyalty to the republic. Finally, six months of rancorous political wrangling ended on 1 October 1928. Defense Minister Groener gave a press conference to announce his selection of Admiral Raeder. Groener had thoroughly examined Captain Gotting's report and decided that Raeder offered the best choice. The press was sympathetic to Groener because he took a liberal position on many issues. However, they demanded clear answers to a trio of questions:

1. While Station Chief at Kiel, Raeder had taken a trip along the Kaiser Wilhelm Canal on the yacht *Nixe* with a group of retired naval officers. Along the way they stopped to sample eels cooked in various restaurants. This social event was an old Imperial Navy custom. The event coincided with Prince Heinrich of Prussia's birthday. Heinrich was absent due to illness but an after-dinner speaker offered a toast to His Royal Highness. How could Raeder loyally command the republic's navy with these imperial associations?

Groener explained that Prince Heinrich was a former grand admiral and shipmate of many guests - including Raeder. Toasting a fellow officer in this social atmosphere seemed appropriate. Anyway, they made the toast ashore and not on a republic-owned vessel.

2. The press wanted clear and specific answers to Raeder's involvement in the Kapp *Putsch:*

Groener pointed out that Raeder was on leave at the time of the *Putsch.* Although he had an important position in the Admiralty, he did not order any illegal arrests. Raeder had faced a parliamentary committee that exonerated him and authorized his further service in the *Reichsmarine.*

3. What about Raeder's ties to right-wing, anti-government groups in the Kiel Station?

The defense minister assured the press that Raeder had ordered all ties severed with such organizations when he assumed his duties in Kiel. Currently, no officer or civilian employee had any tie-in with anti-government groups. An investigation into such activities had taken place after the rebel take over at Kiel. A cynical reporter commented that the investigation had stopped due to an amnesty. Groener covered this with a political answer. The investigation had found nothing to encourage it to continue. Grumbling continued in the press corps but Groener's prestige held any radical objections against Admiral Raeder in check. Groener subsequently appointed him Commander-in-Chief of the *Reichsmarine.*

As navy chief in 1928, Admiral Erich Raeder, had enormous challenges to meet. Noxious residues from the Kapp *Putsch* and the Lohmann Affair still left misgivings in the *Reichstag* against the navy. Political savvy and public relations must concentrate on rescuing the navy from public contempt. The 'sacred duty' to rebuild the High Seas

Fleet must take priority in rearmament discussions.

Raeder swiftly asserted his authority as chief of the navy. In a letter to Admiral von Tirpitz he outlined his basic ideas for the future of the *Reichsmarine*. Admiral Raeder highlighted the political difficulties of getting an adequate share of the military budget. The battleship replacement program could die if the government refused to envision the fleet as a source of prestige. Admiral von Tirpitz congratulated Raeder on his appointment. He shared the view that public opinion favored the army in the military spending. Tirpitz emphasized the vital importance of a fleet to assert Germany's stature in the world community: Any weakening of the nation's resolve to build the *Panzerschiff* would result in an 'irreparable loss of respect before the entire world'. Tirpitz had withdrawn from the *Reichstag* in autumn but Raeder knew he still wielded strong political influence.

While campaigning for C-in-C *Reichsmarine*, Raeder had met Defense Minister Groener at Bad Kreuth. Admiral Raeder clearly outlined his strategy for the future navy. The navy chief must have unrestricted command of the *Marineleitung*, including operations and personnel. He reasoned that the navy chief must have access to all naval discussions in the defense ministry, including those that the navy did not originate. Raeder insisted on independent naval command, free from army influence. All departments, including command, discipline, maintenance and particularly personnel must have singular naval control. This structure created an important precedent in German military command philosophy.

Using this blueprint, Admiral Raeder went to work to recreate the navy in his pre conceived image. Administration problems, inherent in the Imperial Navy, would disappear. In the First World War, the Imperial Naval Cabinet, the Imperial Naval Office and the High Command reported individually to the Kaiser. Raeder felt this caused fragmentation. He decided his new navy must not fall into a similar situation. The navy chief intended to concentrate all questions of policy whether military or administrative in his own hands. Raeder demanded a united naval front against suspicious politicians and a hostile press. He warned that he would not tolerate exposure of naval dissension in any form. The navy must settle conflicts 'in house'. As commander-in-chief, he would retain his prerogatives on every decision. In 1929 the navy issued an official guideline for operations, maneuvers and officer training. This reflected Admiral Raeder's strict demands on the navy and its personnel. Everyone must pull together - the direction and the stroke would come from the C-in-C. Anything less than absolute loyalty to the service and the nation was unacceptable. An Official Service Instruction issued to all commanders clearly defined their responsibility. 'The Commander alone is accountable for his actions to his superiors.'

Self-confidence lived naturally in Erich Raeder. The son of a public school principal, he possessed mental capacity nearly that of a genius. Although physically small, Raeder had a steely toughness of spirit and mind that served him well. A religious family upbringing instilled a strong Lutheran faith that sustained him in many trials throughout his life. His natural leanings toward learning and teaching had given him competence in English, French, Spanish and Russian besides his native tongue. Many published articles and important texts had shown his intelligent use of words and political savvy. A combat hardened naval officer, he earned the respect of his peers and seniors but many subordinates remained distanced. Dour and aloof, without any apparent sense of humor, Admiral Raeder loved his nation and the service. In Raeder's code, the navy and the nation enjoyed a symbiotic relationship. Various governments might take power, then fail, but the navy must stand with the nation.

CHAPTER 9:
Raeder Courts Hitler.

Beginning in 1919, ten bumpy years of the Weimar Republic unfolded. Eight political parties jostled for a leverage position in the *Reichstag* - none held a governing majority. Fifteen consecutive cabinets struggled to make political sense. The basic question of rearmament or disarmament demanded a consensus in the military planning, but it prompted turmoil. In Germany, only the communists (KPD) carried a firmly united policy - they preferred disarmament. Social Democrats (SDP) and the Center Party (Catholic) largely supported disarmament but many dissidents refused to follow the party line. The German National Party (DNVP) believed that Germany must rearm to protect its borders and its interests. Two smaller parties, the German People's Party (DVP) and the German Democratic Party (DDP) advocated peaceful coexistence. At the other extreme, the Bavarian People's Party (BVP) had a separation agenda - they wanted a Bavarian State divorced from the German Empire. National unity in Germany lived in a tenuous environment while most of the population struggled economically to make ends meet.

In January 1919, Anton Dexler and Karl Harrer set up a small political party in Munich. They named it the German Workers Party (DAP). It represented a combined antisemitic and socialist theme. Adolf Hitler dropped into a meeting of this party on 12 September and left as a member of the board. Early in the new year - 24 February - the Party changed its name to the National Socialist German Worker's Party (NSDAP) with Hitler as chief propagandist. In December 1920 this insignificant Nazi party bought the *Voelkischer Beobachter* newspaper to publicize its policies. On 29 July 1921, Hitler emerged as the Nazi party Führer. A prolific hypnotic speaker, Adolf Hitler made thirty-one fiery speeches in one year. To maintain order at Nazi meetings they formed the *Sturmabteilung* (SA) in August 1921. Hitler strongly expatiated that nationalism (unity of the people) and socialism (unity of the state) belonged together.

Germany plunged into hyperinflation in September 1923: one

pound sterling bought fifteen million marks. The nation's reparation payments fell behind and French troops occupied the Ruhr. In passive resistance, Germany halted all coal and iron production. Newly appointed chancellor Gustave Stresemann (DVP) boldly seized the reins of power. First he stabilized the currency - replacing the mark with a strictly controlled *Rentenmark*. The Chancellor then abandoned the passive resistance policy in the Ruhr to end Germany's economic crisis. Adolf Hitler, now a political firebrand, hotly denounced this move.

On 8 November 1923, Bavarian authorities who strongly opposed the Weimar government gathered at the *Burgerbrau Keller* in Munich. Adolf Hitler broke into the meeting with SA forces. Hitler persuaded Gustaf von Kahr (state commissioner), General von Lossow (head of the Bavarian *Reichswehr*) and retired General von Ludendorff to join him in a coup. Later that night Hitler issued a proclamation to replace the existing national government. Next day, Hitler and Ludendorff led a victory march of top Nazi leaders and party members through Munich. But von Kahr and von Lossow had covertly withdrawn their support. Consequently, the *Reichswehr* remained loyal and broke up the Nazi march with a fusillade of gunfire. Two days later, the police arrested Hitler. The courts tried and sentenced him to five years in prison for treason. Hitler served only nine months and in this time he wrote *Mein Kampf*. While Hitler remained in prison, the Nazi Party secured 32 seats in the May election. Then on 7 December 1924, another trip to the polls reduced the Nazi seats to fourteen.

Chancellor Gustav Stresemann soon wrestled the tailspinning economy into reasonable order. Then he moved from chancellor to become foreign secretary. Stresemann took extraordinary pains to live with the Versailles Treaty and negotiated skillfully with the allied victors. The Dawes plan - August 1924 - scaled down the huge reparation payments. A loan to carry the nation over the short term also helped. Later, in December 1925, Stresemann worked out an agreement to settle the border disputes. The Locarno Pact fixed the western boundaries but left the eastern boundaries open to further negotiations. Germany re-entered the world community in 1926 - gaining a seat in the League of Nations. The election in May 1928, showed promise that the Weimar Republic would survive. Chancellor Hermann Müller (SDP) formed a coalition with the smaller moderate parties. The militarist opposition parties had all lost seats. Hitler's Nazis lost further ground, retaining only twelve seats in the *Reichstag*. The fledgling Republican government had miraculously survived a maelstrom of problems. However, Müller's group tended toward disarmament and pacifism. They strongly opposed building the first *Panzerschiff*. Admiral Raeder's dream of a renewed global fleet teetered in the balance.

Then a controversial agreement in 1929 caused tremendous controversy in the *Reichstag* and in the streets. The Young Plan reduced reparation payments but extended the terms to sixty years. Alfred Hugenberg, who had replaced Count Westarp as DNVP party leader in October 1928, organized a massive petition against the Young Plan. This led to a referendum in December. Almost six million votes supported Hugenberg's counter proposal: he rejected recognition of war guilt and refused any new burden of payment. Nevertheless, the party needed 21 million votes to carry the issue. They fell short and lost the referendum. Immediately, German nationalism raged in protest against the iron bonds of Weimar republicanism.

In 1929, Müller's Social Democrats convened a conference to discuss military policy. They agreed to work within the terms of the Treaty of Versailles. Furthermore, they accepted a role in leading the international community, including Germany, toward disarmament. This fired a broadside into German military expectations. The defense ministry demanded rearmament - at least to the levels allowed by the treaty. Admiral Raeder sided with the military's objectives, hoping to snag a proper share of the budget for his Service. The navy C-in-C continued to push his personal agenda on three fronts: internally, to reinvigorate the navy; publicly, to regain national trust; politically, to rebuild a global fleet. Admiral Raeder theorized that the public must understand and appreciate the national importance of a battle fleet. Raeder recognized that national unity came heavily into play. Lacking national acceptance, the navy might inherit a superficial role in the military. This nightmarish possibility must not take place. Admiral von Tirpitz agreed completely with Raeder's philosophy.

Raeder's grim determination to sweep out undesirable elements in the navy had shown quick results. Communists need not apply! A government that purged Bolshevism could rely on Raeder's support. Political infighting that fractured the national interest appalled Raeder.

He prayed for national unity and strived to enable this situation. Candidates who valued a commission in the navy must align with Raeder's conditions. He locked in the criteria of rigid discipline, total obedience and pride in service. Unquestionably, it was Admiral Raeder's navy.

Tirpitz's involvement in the DNVP drew support from mature naval officers. However, this party lacked sufficient numbers to advance a major fleet agenda. On the other hand Hitler's rowdy Nazis had taken nationalism as a creed and blossomed. Raeder hoped that one day Hitler might form a part of the government. He believed that fervent nationalism would benefit the navy's cause. Casting in every direction to further his goals, Raeder sought contact with the still-disreputable Führer. His long time friend Admiral Levetzow had taken the nationalist bait and joined the Nazi Party. Raeder then had a three-way exchange with Hitler beginning in 1928. Using Levetzow as middle man, Raeder kept pace from afar with Hitler's progress and particularly his ideas on naval policy.

In October 1929, a financial disaster struck in New York. The Wall Street crash set the scene for the Great Depression that devastated all industrial nations. Germany had already squeezed the last drop from her economy. Chancellor Müller and his cabinet resigned March 27, 1930: the *Reichstag* had blocked his financial remedies. President Hindenburg called on Heinrich Brüning (Center Party), to form a new government. Brüning decided to balance the budget - whatever the cost. He introduced small tax increases and spending cuts that the *Reichstag* rejected. Chancellor Brüning then invoked an Article 48 amendment, with President Hindenburg's approval, and forced the issue. The *Reichstag* reversed the ploy and struck down the amendment: using the same constitutional article. Consequently, Brüning dissolved the *Reichstag* and governed Germany by Presidential decree. A fiercely contested general election in September 1930, saw a dramatic increase in Nazi seats: from twelve to one-hundred seven. Brüning needed the full support of the SDP and Hindenburg's blessing to govern the nation. Meanwhile, increased unemployment and political uncertainty caused extreme violence in the streets. Hitler's SA and communist *Freikorps* units battled ferociously.

At this time, Defense Minister Groener simultaneously held the interior ministry portfolio. On 13 April 1932, General Groener decided to ban the SA. President Hindenburg signed the approval but bitter protests flooded in from all sides. The exiled Kaiser's sons took part in lobbying Hindenburg to lift the ban. Shortly afterward - 13 May - Groener narrowly won a vote of confidence but resigned as defense minister. Hindenburg then took a hard line on Chancellor Brüning. Word had leaked that the SDP intended pushing legislation to expropriate debt-ridden Prussian estates. On 29 May, Hindenburg withdrew his presidential support from Brüning. Fritz von Papen (Centralist) moved into the chancellor's office on Hindenburg's invitation. Chancellor von Papen worked toward a coalition between Hugenberg (DNVP) and Hitler's Nazis to form a majority. On 9 June, von Papen lifted the ban on the SA. Then on 20 July, he dissolved the SDP Party in Prussia. Nonetheless, Hitler refused Papen's wooing and a mud slinging political battle made busy headlines.

Admiral Raeder anxiously followed the political tussle. In four short years he had used every guile to advance his fleet agenda. Five new light cruisers were already sailing the seas. In the ways, the light cruiser *Nürnberg* progressed daily. Twelve new destroyers proudly carried the flag and Raeder had won the argument in the battleship replacement program - President Hindenburg had launched *Deutschland* in 1931. In the same year the navy laid down a second *Panzerschiff* - *Admiral Scheer*. Furthermore, the *Reichstag* had budgeted two more *Panzerschiffe* for future production. Complying with Raeder's plan, the navy had withdrawn into a shell of pristine public relations. Raeder resolved internally all disruptions that might spot this image. He permitted only positive publicity. In 1931 a young naval officer had compromised the daughter of an important business director. Raeder demanded that the officer marry the young woman. When he refused, Raeder drummed him out of the navy in quick time. Reinhard Heydrich would never forget this humiliation.

Meanwhile, with Levetzow's help, Raeder encouraged increasing friendship with the Nazi Party. In 1932, he tolerated a loose association of a non-political officer's association with the party. Realistically, Raeder must not make an enemy of the burgeoning Nazis. He viewed Hitler's tepid interest and superficial knowledge of naval matters with grave misgivings. When Hitler visited the new cruiser *Koln,* he listened to Raeder's ideas of a new fleet - including battleships. Paradoxically, the

Führer later wrote a scathing attack on von Papen's published naval policy. The Nazi leader stated in *Voelkischer Beobachter* that the planned battleships might endanger Anglo-German relations. Hitler argued: the navy had succumbed to old technology and many younger officers now disagreed with von Papen's policy. Anyway, the money should go to the army. Alarm bells clanged in Raeder's mind - the navy's future might rest on Hitler's whim. The navy C-in-C decided he needed to dissuade Hitler from any thought of a merely coastal fleet. Germany needed a prestigious High Seas Fleet to take her rightful place in international affairs. As Hitler's power grew, Raeder upgraded the importance of the Nazi leader's cooperation.

Ominous changes took place in German politics in 1932. Von Papen failed to get Hitler's support to form a majority and the national government spun in circles. General Kurt von Schleicher, now defense minister, persuaded President Hindenburg that he could form a majority in the *Reichstag*. Von Schleicher hoped to ally with Gregor Strasser who carried a strong following in the Nazi Party. Strasser's ideas ran along strong socialist lines as opposed to Hitler's strident nationalism. Hindenburg switched his support from von Papen and installed von Schleicher as chancellor. Within hours, Hitler furiously accused Strasser of disloyalty and splitting Nazi Party solidarity. Strasser hurriedly retreated from the scene to take a vacation. Hitler successfully demanded affirmation as undisputed party Führer and annexed Strasser's constituency in Berlin.

Chancellor von Schleicher soon resigned and von Papen came back into Hindenburg's favor. Tentative negotiations to renew von Papen's government with Hitler as vice chancellor collapsed. In January 1933, Hindenburg accepted Hitler as chancellor with von Papen as vice chancellor. Hitler also negotiated a new general election and Germany went to the polls in March 1933. Hitler's Nazis won two-hundred and eighty-eight seats: with the cooperation of the DNVP's fifty-two seats, Hitler carried a majority.

Admiral Raeder's concern for his navy's future multiplied. In which direction would Hitler move in naval policy? Hitler's prime military interest centered on the army while his next priority in military expansion favored the air force. Raeder knew he must enlighten the chancellor with the political advantages of a prestigious fleet. Tirpitz had often quoted the 'alliance factor' in naval policy. A powerful German fleet might ally with another nation to achieve political and military leverage. Raeder's political acumen and military status had enabled him to personally contact the top German politicians. Since Groener's resignation he had bypassed incumbent defense ministers and dealt directly with Chancellor Brüning. Now he sought personal negotiation with Hitler.

Admiral Raeder had Hitler's name in his 'enemies of the navy' file. The admiral could revisit every word that the Nazi leader had published or spoken concerning the navy. Raeder intended to emphasize the political significance of an important fleet. Erich Raeder thought he understood Hitler's naval psychosis. Levetzow's exchanges revealed Hitler's contempt for Tirpitz's navy: He had called it a fleet 'built for its own purpose'. Paradoxically, Hitler loved big ships with big guns. Raeder first met Adolf Hitler personally at a dinner party held in General Hammerstein's home. The new chancellor, only a month after his appointment, assured the gathering he would rebuild the armed forces to defend the nation. Further, he stated that SA or SS *Freikorps* units would not impede the national military. Hitler solemnly promised that his program would rout unemployment.

Chancellor Hitler and Admiral Raeder met officially in March 1933. The admiral pressed his point about the 'alliance factor' in a German fleet of battleships and aircraft carriers: international politics valued a prestigious Fleet. It seemed like a concession to the Versailles Treaty to abandon naval expansion. Raeder tried to push all the right buttons. Hitler responded that the army came first. Then Hermann Göring's aircraft production would get a large share of the budget. He remained noncommital on the navy. At the end of the day Raeder feared that Hitler might restrict naval expansion.

In April 1933, the navy launched *Admiral Scheer* and commissioned *Deutschland*. Admiral Raeder poured his soul into rousing speeches that touted the values of a reborn fleet. Hitler insisted on an official visit to the German fleet in May. At Kiel a few weeks later, the *Deutschland* majestically headed a floodlit regatta of every ship in the fleet. Hitler must have felt the beauty and power of the warships - he promised approval of a fourth *Panzerschiffe*.

CHAPTER 10:
War Too Soon.

In 1937, four years of Hitler's mandate had brought Germany new prosperity. The Führer firmly held the reins of power and the National workhorse willingly responded. German self esteem expanded in keeping with well-publicized international achievements in airplanes, ocean liners and sports events. Hitler had set up a four-year plan in September 1936 under Hermann Göring - to further speed the galloping economy. Humming factories that produced world-class industrial products and military hardware soon banished unemployment. Workers received adequate wages and substantial fringe benefits. Dr. Goebbel's Nazi propaganda constantly filled the national news media with positive reports and functions. Young people joined groups to sing the praises of Nazi Germany: The Führer basked in popularity.

On the downside, police control of individual freedoms grew insidiously. Goebbel's propaganda ministry viciously targeted 'racial misfits' and dissidents. They had no qualms and blithely covered up brutal police actions taken against 'enemies of the state'. Also, the minister of economics, Dr. Hjalmar Schacht, resigned in protest to Göring's irresponsible economic strategy.

Hitler's popular book, *Mein Kampf*, had coveted land gains in the east. Now the Führer's unrelenting political agenda rolled toward *Lebensraum*. Germany must annex the areas populated by ethnic German nationals living in Austria, Czechoslovakia and Poland. German troops marched into Austria in March 1938. Then came belligerent confrontations with the Czech government, while troops assembled on her border.

A crossroads in the Nazi leader's planning quickly arrived. Hitler had originally set his mind on cobbling a compromise deal with Great Britain. In 1935 he assumed the naval agreement would help garner British tolerance for a European land grab. Neville Chamberlain had resolved to work with Germany to adjust any 'reasonable' complaints regarding the eastern borders. Hitler decided to risk war against Britain to further his aims.

During political negotiations, the British prime minister quietly demurred in the face of Hitler's bluster. Ultimately Chamberlain patiently negotiated the Munich Agreement. On 30 September 1938, Hitler accepted the return of the *Sudetenland* and agreed to a gradual German occupation. Chamberlain loudly acclaimed this accomplishment of negotiated peace.

Then in March 1939, Germany blatantly occupied the remainder of Czechoslovakia. Hitler immediately lost international credibility and British resolve stiffened. Chamberlain signed an Anglo-French guarantee on 31 March, to defend Poland from aggression. Nevertheless, threat of war with Britain and France did not deter the confident Führer. Hitler firmly believed that Britain would seek a political compromise if Germany quickly overran Poland. Admiral Raeder knew of Hitler's aggressive intentions as they progressed. Yet he believed that Hitler would magically weave a political web to achieve his aims. So far, a combination of threats and promises had produced amazing results without a major war. Hitler again reassured Raeder he would not go to war against Great Britain. Still, Raeder and many army generals nervously analyzed Hitler's program of conquest. General Beck had resigned to protest the invasion of Czechoslovakia. The army generals claimed they could not support a major war. Privately, some high ranking generals had quietly planned to capture Hitler and seize the government. British intelligence agents had contacted the plotters. However, vigilant Gestapo actions eliminated these prospects.

Erich Raeder had labored doggedly for twenty years to resurrect the High Seas Fleet. He clearly envisioned a world-class navy and a strategy to use it. Raeder believed that modern warfare must blend coordinated military actions with economics and politics, on a global scale. Heroic 'in-line' sea-battles between opposing capital ships had slipped into history. Global war tactics must concentrate on an economic war. Predictably, Raeder's *Kriegsmarine* would play a leading role.

Admiral Erich Raeder lacked neither insight nor confidence. The navy C-in-C had presented a case for battleships in his early bid to win Hitler's support. Adolf Hitler admired the incredible firepower inherent in a massive battleship. Raeder strongly stressed the 'alliance principle' in his arguments, the idea that a modern fleet with great battleships could promote political advantage secured Hitler's blessing.

Concurrently, political problems in the First World War had relegated submarines to a secondary role.

When the Z-Plan graduated to the drawing boards Raeder wanted fast cruisers that could outrun enemy capital ships with bigger guns. Conversely, his battle cruisers must have heavier guns than enemy ships with equal speed. Plus, the navy C-in-C strongly advocated the importance of aircraft carriers and battleships. Raeder envisioned a submarine arm that would serve inshore duties - not oceangoing combat vessels. Admiral Raeder pictured a fleet of cruisers and battle cruisers raiding enemy commerce on the high seas. Using a 'two-pole' tactic they would attack widely different locations. To counter this tactic the enemy must spread its available defenses over a large area. Hitler did not agree with Raeder's 'two-pole' naval strategy. The Führer demanded the biggest possible battleships with the biggest possible guns in his future fleet. It seemed that Hitler would cancel the Z-Plan if they excluded big battleships. Raeder gently complained but compromised with little remorse

During 1939 Raeder ordered six H-Class battleships (56,000 tons) and three O-Class battle cruisers (32,000 tons). They designed these new warships for speeds over 33 knots. The battleships mounted eight 16-inch guns and the battle cruisers had six 15-inch guns. An ingenious combination of diesel and steam turbine engines would give the battle cruisers flexible speed and range. Powerful new diesel engines would drive the battleships. Busy German shipyards resounded with urgent activity. Two new battle cruisers had already joined the fleet - *Gneisenau* on 21 May, 1938, and *Scharnhorst on* 7 January, 1939. Meanwhile, work rapidly advanced on the battleships *Bismarck* and *Tirpitz*. *Graf Zeppelin*, Germany's first aircraft carrier, took her place in the frenzied building program. Designers also drew up plans to convert two passenger vessels and the heavy cruiser *Seydlitz* into aircraft carriers. Göring had promised in 1935 to deliver 700 aircraft for service on the carriers but continually reneged on his promise.

Chancellor Hitler had eagerly previewed *Bismarck* in November 1938 - before her launch. Disappointed and angry, the Führer criticized the battleship's design and combat ability. This caused a blazing row between Raeder and Hitler that prompted the admiral to offer his resignation. No sign of this exchange appeared on 14 February 1939, when they launched *Bismarck*. Every leading Nazi Party member joined Hitler and Raeder to praise Germany's new battleship - immodestly rated the world's best. Göring, Goebbels, Hess, Ribbentrop, Himmler, and Bormann all smiled and congratulated the navy's accomplishment. Still, Raeder's constant politicking for more naval funding soured relations within the power structure. Göring and Himmler developed a bitter animosity against Raeder and his navy.

Göring had multiplied Raeder's problems concerning control of naval aircraft. In January 1939, the Luftwaffe took over all aspects of naval aviation. This included minelaying, reconnaissance and aircraft attack on shipping. Provision of aircraft and their crews for the intended aircraft carriers depended solely on the Luftwaffe. The navy controlled the design and construction of seaplanes but the Luftwaffe supplied, maintained and crewed the machines. Nonetheless, Hitler appreciated Raeder's total dedication to the nation and the navy. At this time he left naval concerns in Raeder's hands. Hitler ran the army, Göring ran the air-force, Himmler ran the police, and Raeder ran the navy. Admiral Raeder enthusiastically charged ahead with his construction program. The C-in-C Navy used every wile to short circuit delays. However, submarine research and development continued in the shade.

On 1 April, Admiral von Tirpitz's granddaughter, Frau von Hassel, launched the battleship *Tirpitz*. Hitler then promoted Admiral Raeder to grand admiral. The Führer effusively praised the new grand admiral for his wonderful work with the navy over many years. He again assured Raeder 'clearly and definitely' that he would not provoke Britain into war before completion of the Z-Plan. Spring exercises in the Atlantic, grouped *Admiral Graf Spee* and *Deutschland* with three cruisers and a flotilla of destroyers. Captain Hans Langsdorff commanded *Admiral Graf Spee* in the training program. The British Royal Navy showed little concern for the German warships. A cross-channel steamer casually gave notice of the German activity.

Suddenly, on 28 April, Hitler unilaterally abrogated the Anglo-German Naval Agreement. The Führer threw the gauntlet into Britain's face in a speech to the *Reichstag* - without advising Raeder. Undaunted, the grand admiral continued to publicly promote the navy and the importance of battleships. At Brunswick on 20 May, Raeder addressed an assembly of the Hitler Youth Movement. The grand admiral loudly proclaimed, *"Battleships alone are able to win or defend the supremacy of the seas."* Shortly afterwards, the shipbuilders Blohm and Voss laid down the gigantic keel plates for battleship 'H' in Hamburg. One month later - 15 August - A.G. Weser laid the plates for battleship 'J' in Bremen. Raeder was rushing to tie down his budgeted funds and comply with Hitler's demands.

Paradoxically, storm clouds gathered in the naval ranks. Captain Karl Dönitz, despite his new promotion on 1 January, grumbled about the low priority given to his submarine force. Construction of new vessels crawled forward at a snail's pace. Complaints of serious flaws in torpedo mechanisms dropped out of sight into a bureaucratic swamp. Grand Admiral Raeder paid lip service to Dönitz. Raeder assured him that they had included sufficient submarine requirements in the Z-Plan. Time would correct any temporary imbalance in the fleet mix.

On 22 July, the navy C-in-C confidently addressed the U-boat officers. He assured them that the Führer had pledged to avoid an early war with Britain. Hitler had continually argued that Britain would find a political excuse to renege on its guarantees to Poland. Admiral Raeder fervently hoped they could avoid war. Yet, with a completed Z-Plan - in 1946 - Raeder would gladly challenge the Royal Navy. Still, Hitler's intention to invade Poland caused the admiral to reassess the navy's fortunes. Raeder did not share the Führer's optimism. The admiral's glowing vision of a reborn German fleet began to dim.

Knowing that Hitler intended to attack Poland on 1 September, Raeder prayed that the Führer would pull off another political miracle. Nevertheless, the navy C-in-C prudently issued orders in August to place the pocket battleships and submarines at strategic war stations.

Admiral Graf Spee left Wilhelmshaven, equipped for war duties, on 21 August 1939. The supply ship *Altmark* would join her in the South Atlantic. Three days later, *Deutschland* sailed to take up her station in the mid Atlantic - *Westerwald* would provision this pocket battleship. Between 19 and 21 August, eighteen submarines took positions to the north and north west, off Great Britain. Three submarines remained in the Baltic.

The grand admiral issued top-secret operational orders for *Deutschland* and *Admiral Graf Spee* on 4 August 1939. The details filled several pages. A political segment surmised that Britain and France would support Poland. Raeder expected Italy as a German ally with additional support from Spain and Japan. Russia would likely remain neutral. Germany must respect the neutrality of all nations at sea until the combatants declared official war zones. Under a subheading *'Tasks in the Event of War'* the orders specified:

> *"Disruption and destruction of enemy merchant ships by all possible means."* For this the following is ordered:
>
> (a) *Merchant warfare is, in the beginning, to be waged according to Prize Law.*
>
> (b) *If in the beginning or during the course of the war Germany declares 'danger zones' then unrestricted warfare is permitted in these areas. To avoid attacks from our own U-boats due to mistaken identity, pocket battle ships are to keep out of 'danger zones' unless special areas are named.*
>
> (c) *Enemy naval forces, even if inferior, are only to be engaged if it should further the principal task(i.e., war on merchant shipping).*
>
> (d) *Frequent changes of position in the operational areas will create uncertainty and will restrict enemy merchant shipping, even without tangible results. A temporary departure into distant areas will also add to the uncertainty of the enemy.*
>
> (e) *If the enemy should protect his shipping with superior forces so that direct success cannot be obtained, then the mere fact that his shipping is so restricted means that we have greatly impaired his supply situation. Valuable results will also be obtained if the pocket battleships continue to remain in the convoy area.*
>
> (f) *The enemy is not in a position to carry his complete import requirements in escorted convoys. Independent ships can therefore be expected.*

Adolf Hitler continued to weigh the odds against Britain holding fast to defend Poland. Meeting with senior generals on 22 August, he repeated: *"I believe it is impossible that a responsible English statesman - given this situation - would incur the risk of war."* Simultaneously, von Ribbentrop courted Stalin and Molotov in Moscow. Next day - 23 August - they signed the Soviet-German Non-Aggression Treaty. A fresh breeze of confidence swept through the German military. Perhaps the Führer had the situation well in hand.

Germany conducted her first Blitzkrieg on 1 September 1939. Shells and bombs rained down on Poland like a hellish hurricane. Tanks and infantry joined the action and brushed through Poland with devastating firepower. An ancient battleship - *Schleswig-Holstein* - battered Westerplatte with 11-inch shells. The defending Poles held out for seven days, then the fortress near Danzig surrendered. In Britain on 3 September Parliament declared war against Germany. France also declared war to fulfill the Polish accord.

CHAPTER 11:

Battleships v U-boats v Bombers.

Britain's declaration of war in September 1939 devastated Admiral Raeder. Victory over Britain meant cutting her sea borne supply lines. During the First World War unrestricted use of U-boats had ravaged enemy shipping but raised unprecedented political problems. Accordingly, Admiral Raeder's grandiose fleet plans had left the U-boat division in a low priority - he had concentrated on building a powerful surface fleet.

In direct contradiction Vice Admiral Dönitz had submitted a concise memorandum to naval high command in August 1939. C-in-C submarines claimed he needed 300 U-boats to pose any threat to Britain. Dönitz strongly suggested they muster every resource to build these without delay. War against Britain now pinpointed the U-boat as Germany's premier naval weapon but only fifty-seven submarines were in service. Conversely, capital ship production reached record-breaking levels. Two heavy battleships - *Bismarck* and *Tirpitz* - neared completion. In addition, the shipyards had laid down the massive keel plates of two 56,000 ton "H" class battleships. Besides this battleship activity, work on the aircraft carrier *Graf Zeppelin* advanced daily. Admiral Raeder's booming Z-Plan promised much more.

Nevertheless, German capital-ship strength currently totaled two battle cruisers - *Scharnhorst* and *Gneisenau* - and three pocket battleships. Two new heavy cruisers - *Hipper* and *Blücher* - backed up the capital ships and *Prinz Eugen,* another heavy cruiser, would soon join the fleet. Comparing his meager navy against the allied armada, Raeder glumly stated that German naval forces could only "die gallantly."

In 1894, Erich Raeder had joined the navy. He was an intellectual youth, at eighteen. Young Raeder grew to manhood within the Kaiser's imperial navy. Throughout the First World War he served with courage and distinction in Admiral von Hipper's elite battle cruiser squadron. At the Battle of Jutland, Raeder experienced fierce front-line action. After the war, Raeder survived the political and physical destruction of the imperial fleet. In 1928 he battled against strong opposition to become C-in-C of the fledgling *Reichsmarine*. Raeder then worked devotedly to build a credible German battle fleet. When war began in 1939, Admiral Raeder held dictatorial control of the expanding *Kriegsmarine*. Only the Führer had more power over the navy and Hitler cared little about naval warfare. The calculating navy chief believed he had Hitler's measure. For several years Raeder had patiently persuaded Adolf Hitler that battleships held the key to naval power. Raeder argued that big battleships could accrue political leverage. Alternately, he allowed that U-boats carried a malodorous political stigma from the First World War. Now, plunged into a premature war, Raeder approached the chancellor with a new plea. Vice Admiral Dönitz's demand for 300 U-boats carried special merit. Raeder requested additional naval funds and materials to provide the necessary U-boats.

Hitler agreed with Raeder's presentation but adamantly refused *additional* resources for the navy. Germany had a crucial shortage of zinc and other war materials. They had focused the nation's energies to enlarge the army and the air force. Raeder's navy must live within its budget and wait for another day. The Führer also imposed some restrictions on Raeder's war strategy. During the first weeks of the war Hitler banned 'unrestricted use' of submarines. In addition he placed a restraint on the surface raiders. They must not attack enemy merchant ships unless in defense. Poland now lay in ruins and Hitler confidently expected a deal with Britain to avoid all-out war. Admiral Raeder disagreed with Hitler's assessment. Prime Minister Chamberlain could not compromise again. Munich had driven home a bitter lesson. In the admiral's view, the navy should immediately attack the enemy's shipping before they could take defensive measures. A swift punishing naval offensive might force Britain into a bargaining disposition.

As the prospects of peace faded, Hitler adjusted his hold on the surface raiders. On 29 September, he loosed the pocket battleships against British merchant ships but excluded French vessels. Hitler considered that a political compromise might still sideline France from the war.

At the end of September, two pocket battleships began operations. *Graf Spee* raided in the South Atlantic and *Deutschland* patrolled above the equator. *Admiral Scheer*, the third pocket battleship, lay in

Wilhelmshaven undergoing extensive modifications. Operational instructions issued to *Deutschland* and *Graf Spee* on 4 August 1939, forbade them to engage in action against enemy warships *'even if inferior.'* But a proviso - *'unless to further the disruption of trade'* - made the orders malleable. The ships' commanders had an ambiguous assignment. Disrupt merchant trade by all means, but don't take risks.

In prewar days, Admiral Raeder had critically analyzed the command structure of the imperial navy. Various equally ranked departments had reported directly to the Kaiser. This often caused confusion in operations. Striving to optimize fleet operations, Raeder introduced a new command system. Overall control of naval affairs rested with the *Oberkommando der Kriegsmarine* (OKM) in Berlin. Control of sea operations flowed from the *Seekriegsleitung* (SKL), also stationed in Berlin. To direct daily operations Raeder set up two shore-based command posts. Naval Group West (Wilhelmshaven) directed the North Sea area and Naval Group East (Kiel) handled the Baltic. Admiral Raeder ruled supreme at the head of OKM and SKL in Berlin - he answered only to Hitler.

This change in structure soon stirred resentment between the fleet commanders and the shore-based group commanders. Admiral Boehm, fleet commander of the battle cruisers, angrily complained that Group West reduced his freedom of action. Bitter exchanges between Boehm and Admiral Saalwächter in Wilhelmshaven led to Boehm's resignation. Raeder supported Saalwächter's seniority in the disagreement and replaced Boehm with Vice Admiral Marschall. Grand Admiral Raeder, C-in-C *Kriegsmarine,* absolutely ruled the roost.

Raeder's war strategy sought to simultaneously attack the enemy in widely separated locations. He must force the royal navy to spread their defenses over a huge area. On 7 October he sent *Gneisenau* with nine destroyers on a diversionary sortie while mine layers seeded Britain's east coast. Sixty-six freighters and three destroyers eventually went to the bottom from this operation. Meanwhile, German U-boats had shown their importance in the war. They sank 39 allied ships in September - including the aircraft carrier *Courageous* and five tankers. Admiral Raeder's small, potent navy would bravely give its all in the cause of the fatherland. Erich Raeder strongly believed that valiant naval action, even in defeat, would seed a gallant rebirth of the *Kriegsmarine* in a post war era.

Taking advantage of the U-boat successes, Raeder asked Hitler for priority to build twenty-five U-boats per month. Hitler supported the idea but still refused to authorize *additional* resources to the navy. To free up some resources for submarine production, Raeder was forced to stop work on the 'H' and 'J' battleships. Then he withdrew two of the remaining four orders for the same class warship. Meanwhile, orders for three new 32,000 ton battle cruisers remained in limbo. Conversely, the admiral cracked the whip to complete the two emerging battleships. *Bismarck* entered service in August 1940 and *Tirpitz* five months later. Despite a smouldering feud with Göring over supplying aircraft, the navy chief poured scarce materials into the aircraft carrier *Graf Zeppelin*. Relative trickles of men and materials dribbled through the submarine-building system and the Z-Plan faded into wishful dreams.

In October 1939, Admiral Raeder reviewed the strategic hardships facing the German navy in wartime. Major problems arose from the geographic location of its home ports. Access to the Atlantic required avoiding vigilant enemy patrols. German naval strategy for many years had coveted a secure naval base in Norway to reduce this problem. Raeder presented this thought to Hitler at their naval conference on 10 October. The admiral suggested they should assure the Norwegian routing of vital iron ore shipments from Sweden plus get naval bases. He argued that Britain might land troops in Norway to interdict the ore supplies.

The Führer listened distractedly to Raeder's submission. Four days prior - on 6 October - the dictator had revealed his immediate intentions in a rousing speech. Hitler wanted peace with Britain but threatened that Britain's refusal could generate a world war - 'fought till the bitter end'. An ominous British silence had greeted Hitler's bombastic speech.

But the Führer's longing for *Lebensraum* would not wait for British blessings. Preoccupied with an itch to attack France and the Low Countries he paid scant attention to Raeder's suggestion about Norway. Undeterred by Hitler's tepid response, Admiral Raeder met with Vidkun Quisling in Berlin on 11 October. The Norwegian fascist leader asked for protection against Russian aggression. Quisling guaranteed naval bases in Norway if he attained power and Raeder apprized Hitler accordingly. The Führer appreciated the advantages of a 'friendly occupation' of Norway, but he did not wish to antagonize Russia. However, he authorized Raeder to investigate all Norwegian possibilities through OKM.

So far, the Führer had allowed Admiral Raeder to manage the navy with little interference. Then an incident involving a pocket battleship drew Hitler's attention. On 8 October, *Deutschland* stopped and boarded an American freighter on the high seas. Captain Wennecker ordered his prize crew to take *City of Flint* to Murmansk and thence to Germany. But angry protests from the United States caused the merchant ship to put into a Norwegian port. The neutral Norwegians interned the prize crew and returned the ship to her original owners. Hitler immediately ordered Raeder to bring *Deutschland* home. He feared the propaganda effects if the enemy sank this high-profile warship. *Deutschland* arrived in Gydnia on 15 November where they changed her name to *Lützow*. Germany now had only one surface raider in the South Atlantic - the *Graf Spee*. Raeder's clever two-pole naval strategy suffered accordingly.

About this time, a huge propaganda boost for submarines filled the headlines. On 13 October, Günther Prien's *U-47* entered Scapa Flow and sank the British battleship HMS *Royal Oak*. Prien escaped without damage. Three days of festivities in Berlin featured the U-boat ace. Admiral Raeder's ongoing appeal for more U-boats gained more approval, but still without additional materials or funds.

Meanwhile, OKM had drawn up naval plans for an 'economic war'. Admiral Raeder theorized that global war required the coordination of all services. The navy, army, and air force must tie in with the political agenda - under one command - to attain maximum effect. Raeder presented this strategy to Hitler on 23 October. Hitler liked the idea and authorized a special staff set up in OKM toward this end. Coincidentally, combined operations offered the best chance of a successful military move against Norway.

On 20 November, Hitler issued *Weisung #9* - a plan for economic warfare. To gain victory against the enemy the navy must work in cooperation with the air force. Operational command would lie in the hands of either force depending on circumstances. In practice, personal differences and ambitions between Göring and Raeder frustrated the plan. This animosity continued throughout the war.

Admiral Raeder believed the navy should carry out his theories in an 'economic war'. Facing an overwhelming naval adversary, the admiral planned to attack on a global front, avoiding 'unnecessary' risks. Continuous operations targeting widely dispersed areas would compensate for the German navy's paucity of warships. To prove this idea OKM planned a sortie with Vice Admiral Marschall's two battle cruisers. Marschall would patrol south of Iceland and strike inferior forces to maintain pressure on the North Atlantic sea routes. Simultaneously, *Graf Spee* would raid merchant shipping in the South Atlantic.

Gneisenau and *Scharnhorst* with cruisers *Köln* and *Leipzig* left Wilhelmshaven on 21 November. Three destroyers, *Bernd von Arnim, Karl Glaster, Erich Giese* and three torpedo boats sailed in company. Next day they detached all the light forces to return to the Skaggerak. On 24 November, the small ships linked with the pocket battleship *Lützow* and made a diversionary sweep into the North Sea.

Meanwhile, the two German battle cruisers, flying British white ensigns, beat a harried course northward through hurricane strength gales. With speed sometimes reduced to 12 knots, they headed for the Iceland-Faeroes passage. Suddenly, a signal from *Scharnhorst* on 23 November alerted Marschall, *'have sighted large steamer on parallel course.' Scharnhorst* immediately moved to intercept the steamer with *Gneisenau* in her wake. *Rawalpindi*(16,697btr), was a former passenger liner fitted with 6-inch guns as an auxiliary cruiser. Vice Admiral Marschall gave fair warning but soon opened fire. Captain Kennedy sent a wireless signal at 17:03: **'under attack by *Deutschland'*[sic]**. A thirty-minute bombardment with 11-inch armament soon reduced the auxiliary cruiser to a burning, sinking wreck.

HMS *Newcastle*, had picked up *Rawalpindi's* transmission. At 18:17 the 8-inch-gun cruiser sent a message: **'have sighted cruiser *Deutschland* [sic] distance 13,000 yds.'** Immediately afterward, at 18:18 she signaled: *'lights of second ship . . . . approaching from dead ahead.'* In London, the Admiralty picked up the signals. The first lord, Churchill, and Admiral Pound monitored the situation from the Admiralty war room. Northern patrol cruisers *Newcastle* and *Delhi* were closing the Germans' position. Also, HMS *Hood* and *Dunkerque* steered a course northward to cut off the enemies' return to Germany.

From Kiel, shore-based Group West signaled Marschall that the cruisers *Delhi* and *Newcastle*, plus capital warships from the Home Fleet had his scent. Shortly afterwards, while rescuing survivors, the Germans sighted *Newcastle*. Marschall immediately threw out a smokescreen and turned away to escape. He headed northward toward the Arctic and outran *Newcastle* in severe weather. A meteorological report had forecast storm conditions along the Norwegian coast. Taking advantage of terrible weather, Marschall brought his two battle cruisers back to Wilhelmshaven on 27 November.

German headlines applauded 'A Great Naval Victory Off Iceland.' However, Admiral Raeder would not allow specific mention of Vice Admiral Marschall or his ships. Best the enemy continues to blame *Deutschland*.

Paradoxically, the apparent hero came under heavy criticism from SKL. Vice Admiral Fricke (SKL chief of operations) complained that Marschall had not fulfilled his orders - to maintain strategic pressure on the North Atlantic shipping lanes. Fricke scorned Marschall for running away from the cruiser *Newcastle*. "Battleships are supposed to shoot - not lay smokescreens," he complained.

Vice Admiral Marschall strongly objected to such criticism from the High Command. Marschall claimed that without destroyers in company he could not risk a night action against the British cruiser. Marschall insisted he could not afford damage to either of his ships - Germany had only two battle cruisers. Still, SKL remained unhappy with Marschall's performance and Hitler had some strong words for Raeder. Angrily, the Führer commented that he was unaware of the battle cruisers' mission. Then he unkindly scoffed at the huge risk with small return in Marschall's sortie.

Hitler's rising interest in the navy promised future aggravation for Admiral Raeder. Fortunately, Raeder's interest in Norway received a positive boost. Russia suddenly attacked Finland in November. Would British troops now enter and pass through Norway to aid Finland? Raeder arranged a meeting between Hitler and Quisling on 14 December. This resulted in Hitler requesting a feasibility study from the *Oberkommando der Wehrmacht* (OKW) to invade Norway.

Tally Ho!

CHAPTER 12:
Hunting the German Raiders.

During September 1939, the British Admiralty expected immediate raider attacks in the sea lanes. Anxious weeks passed without incident until the last day of the month. Then a German pocket battleship attacked SS *Clement* off Pernambuco, Brazil. The raider took the British captain and chief engineer prisoners aboard, while the merchant's crew escaped in the ship's lifeboats. Then the warship sank the freighter. A few days later - 5 October - the pocket battleship *Deutschland* sank SS *Stonegate* between Bermuda and Madeira. Two pocket battleships at large in the Atlantic called for immediate countermeasures. Admiral Sir Dudley Pound, First Sea Lord, quickly organized cruisers and capital ships into eight hunting groups to protect the sea lanes. This involved twenty-three vessels.

Vice Admiral George D'Oyly Lyon, based in Freetown, figured strongly in Admiral Pound's strategy. As C-in-C South Atlantic, he controlled four hunting groups. They covered the vast seas encompassed within Cape Town and Freetown in West Africa and Pernambuco and Port Stanley in South America. Forces 'G' 'H' and 'M' consisted of three pairs of 8-inch-gun cruisers. Force 'K' comprised the aircraft carrier HMS *Ark Royal* and the battle cruiser HMS *Renown*. Wireless signals between the ships and the Admiralty underpinned Lyon's task. October 1939 brought anxious times for D'Oyly Lyon's South Atlantic Task Force. Four merchant ships had failed to show at their destinations.

On 15 November, a pocket battleship attacked the tanker *Africa Shell* off Portuguese East Africa. D'Oyly Lyon spent great effort seeking the elusive raider without success. Eventually - 2 December - SS *Port Chalmers* intercepted a wireless signal at 12:49: **"RRR RRR RRR 19°15' S; 05°05' E; Doric Star *gunned, battleship*."** *Port Chalmers* rebroadcast this message using her own call sign and Captain Higgs listened for a reaction. This came after midnight when Walvis Bay in South Africa relayed *Doric Star's* distress signal. Next morning, at 05:01 *Port Chalmers* wireless operators intercepted a garbled signal announcing another surface raider attack. *"RRR 21°20 south 320, battleship von Scheer."*

Port Chalmers again relayed the message into the ether. At 15:30 Simonstown signaled to the Admiralty and to Vice Admiral D'Oyly Lyon in Freetown. The station reported positions of an enemy battleship running amok in the South Atlantic. The news immediately triggered a sequence of actions.

Admiral Pound had previously advised D'Oyly Lyon that Force 'I' (HMS *Dorsetshire, Cornwall and Eagle*) was steaming from Ceylon and nearing Madagascar. They would hold course and patrol off the Cape of Good Hope. D'Oyly Lyon ordered the cruisers HMS *Sussex* and *Shropshire* to precede *Ark Royal* and *Renown* to the Cape of Good Hope. After fueling, the cruisers would cover the sea route from the Cape of Good Hope to Saint Helena. Uncertain of the raider's intentions, Lyon signaled Admiral Pound that she might come south east into the Indian Ocean. The First Sea Lord immediately rejected this idea and insisted that Lyon plan on protecting the Atlantic. *Ark Royal* and *Renown* (Force 'K') refueled at the Cape of Good Hope. D'Oyly Lyon ordered them to join the cruisers west of *Doric Star's* last reported position. Rear Admiral Wells, the Flag Officer Commanding, suggested they might better take a position in mid-Atlantic. This left a choice of reaching Freetown, Rio de Janeiro or the Falklands. Vice Admiral D'Oyly Lyon concurred. Lyon then seconded his 6-inch-gun cruiser, HMS *Neptune*, to Force 'X'(*Dupliex, Foch and HMS Hermes*) covering the narrows between Pernambuco and Freetown. The French group should step up patrols in this vital area from 10 December. Finally, the Admiralty diverted the submarine HMS *Severn* to Trinidad from her present course toward the Falklands. Four powerful hunting groups and a submarine combined their efforts to find and destroy the pocket battleship. Admiral Raeder's strategic 'two pole' policy was working as intended.

British naval intelligence also played a role. A small group of naval officers, the Consular Shipping Advisory Department, had set up in Montevideo to monitor British shipping in South America. Captain Hammond RN commanded the unit and Commander H.D. Johnson RN supervised intelligence activities. Since a sea battle in the Atlantic seemed imminent, Commander Johnson arranged a pause in British merchants sailing from Montevideo.

Meanwhile, Commodore Henry Harwood, commanding the South

American Cruiser Division, studied the signals reporting two sequential raider attacks. Harwood minutely calculated the date, time and recorded positions of the attacked merchants. Carefully, he figured the course and speed of the pocket battleship and concluded she might arrive in his area on 12 or 13 December. Would she come to the Plate or Rio de Janeiro? A possible attack on the Falklands naval base also loomed. The anniversary of the Battle of the Falklands - 8 December 1914 - lay close. Land-based volunteers had already set up defenses to resist any surprise attack.

Commodore Harwood commanded four cruisers. HMS *Cumberland* and *Exeter* carried 8-inch guns and HMS *Ajax* and *Achilles* mounted 6-inch guns. This small division patrolled the enormous Atlantic coast of South America. Unfortunately, Harwood's heaviest ship, *Cumberland*, now urgently needed maintenance. Henry 'Bobby' Harwood had long theorized that two 8-inch-gun cruisers could neutralize a pocket battleship. Many of his peers strongly disagreed. Harwood maintained that a simultaneous attack on opposite sides of a pocket battleship could inflict laming damage. But would this conclusion obtain when using one 8-inch-gun cruiser and two 6-inch-gunned cruisers? Furthermore, where would the raider strike? Every naval instinct and sensibility pointed to his most vulnerable area - the River Plate.

On 3 December Commodore Harwood signaled instructions to his ships:

> *In view of a reported pocket battleship* **Cumberland** *to proceed to Port Stanley and remain ready to sail even while under repairs. The oiler RFA* **Olynthus** *will remain in the River Plate area.* **Ajax**, **Achilles** *and* **Exeter** *will concentrate 250 miles off Uruguay. Strict radio silence after this message.*

On 5 December, Vice Admiral Lyon signaled Harwood: the 8-inch-gun cruiser HMS *Dorsetshire* would arrive at Port Stanley on 23 December to replace *Exeter*. Commodore Harwood had earlier suggested a 10,000 ton cruiser might relieve *Exeter*. Lyon's message was the last recorded signal between Lyon and Harwood before the Battle of the River Plate. Complying with Harwood's directions, the three cruisers now comprising Force 'G' met off Uruguay on 12 December. They had silenced wireless activity and cautiously withheld aircraft reconnaissance. Commodore Harwood signaled precise instructions to his Division:

> *My policy with three cruisers in company versus one pocket battle-ship. Attack at once by day or night. By day as two units. 1st Division (Ajax and Achilles) and Exeter diverged to permit flank marking. By night ships will normally remain in company in open order. Be prepared for the signal ZMM, which is to have the same meaning as MM* except that for Division read single ship.*

Later, to ensure complete understanding, the Commodore amplified his message:

> *My object in the signal ZMM is to avoid torpedoes and take the enemy by surprise and cross his stern. Without further orders ships are to clear the line of fire by hauling astern of the leading ship. The new leading ship is to lead the line without further orders so as to maintain decisive gun range.*

In the evening, the ships practiced the manoeuver until perfect. They also exercised fire concentration and flank marking. Crews went to their bunks tired but confident. Meanwhile, the vast resources of the royal navy listened tensely across the immense space of the South Atlantic. Where and when would the German pocket battleship appear? No one could guess that the South American cruiser division would make naval history within the next few hours.

---

*MM - Commanders of Divisions are to turn their Divisions to course . . . starting with rear Division.

Hitler visits the Kreigsmarine   — JOSEPH GILBEY

Hitler returns to Shore   — Joseph Gilbey

Pocket Battleship Deutschland
in Mediterranean (1937)
— Joseph Gilbey

Deutschland *Bombed in Spanish Civil War*

Pocket Battleship Admiral Scheer bombards Almeria — JOSEPH GILBEY

Deutschland Casualties Memorial

Admiral Graf Spee Casualties Buried in Montevideo (1939) — JOSEPH GILBEY

Tombs in Cementerio del Norte Montevideo

Langsdorff Sprinkles Earth onto each Coffin — Joseph Gilbey

Captain Langsdorff Speaking in Montevideo — JOSEPH GILBEY

Captain Langsdorff Salutes his Fallen Men   — JOSEPH GILBEY

114

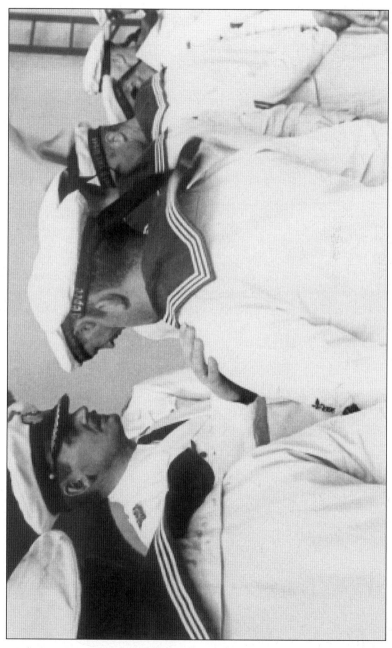

Captain Langsdorff and his Crew   — Joseph Gilbey

Captain Hans Langsdorff and his Family   — JOSEPH GILBEY

CHAPTER 13:
Captain Langsdorff's Dilemma.

Rocking gently on a mid-Atlantic swell 25 November, *Graf Spee* rendezvoused with her supply ship *Altmark*. Captain Langsdorff had captured *Africa Shell* ten days earlier off Mozambique. They shelled and beached the little tanker before meeting *Altmark* in mid-Atlantic. *Africa Shell* marked the sixth prize the German raider had taken within two months. Captain Langsdorff followed the Hague Conventions scrupulously - without causing any loss of life. After sinking a prize, Langsdorff ran *Graf Spee* quickly to a new location in the vast Atlantic. Enemy hunting groups could not pin him down, let alone bring him to action. Conversely, excellent intelligence from Berlin and her own radio experts enabled *Graf Spee* to identify and avoid danger. But Captain Langsdorff now faced a crucial decision.

Graf Spee had left Wilhelmshaven on 21 August. Maintenance recommendations for the Man diesel engines required a dock overhaul every one-thousand hours. *Spee's* eight diesels had labored non stop almost double this time. Three months' constant running had produced serious mechanical problems. *Graf Spee* urgently needed extensive dock maintenance.

Spee's engine mechanics had carefully nursed their charges but excessive vibration had split fifteen auxiliary engine supports. Consequently, one cracked piston and some out-of-round cylinders caused problems in the main engines. Twelve pistons needed ring replacements - for the second time. *Graf Spee's* maximum speed had dropped from 26 knots to 23 knots. Every turn of her screws worsened the condition. Also, unavoidable smoke emissions could betray their presence over the horizon. High Command had previously planned a major overhaul for February 1940.

Lying in company with his supply ship, Captain Langsdorff carefully analyzed the situation. Unquestionably, *Spee* could not continue raiding as previously. The westward route home took him across the Atlantic toward South America, then a northern course through the 'narrows' between Freetown and Pernambuco. A new moon at the end of January offered the best hope of avoiding enemy patrols.

Langsdorff knew from wireless intelligence that the Force 'G' hunting group patrolled the coast of South America. Two heavy cruisers carrying 8-inch guns led the group. Then two 6-inch light cruisers completed the division - perhaps with help from two destroyers and two submarines. Berlin intelligence had reported that British warships escorted freighters out of the River Plate and Rio de Janeiro. Captain Langsdorff had specifically identified the enemy warships and their qualities. *Graf Spee* had captured the British merchant ship *Huntsman* on 10 October. *Spee's* prize crew discovered a copy of a special wireless instruction to British hunting groups:

1. *Don't scatter naval forces. Protect main merchant points of concentration.*
2. *Separate shipping lanes by 100 miles.*
3. *Don't lose time searching in open waters if position of enemy unknown. Weigh probability of success with danger of neglecting more important tasks.*

Langsdorff's general operational orders, issued on 4 August 1939 to the pocket battleships, disallowed any combat with enemy warships: *'Enemy naval forces, even if inferior, are only to be engaged if it should further the principal task(i.e., war on merchant shipping)'*.

Now faced with deteriorating engines, Langsdorff weighed a serious decision. Should he abort the raiding cruise and unobtrusively sneak home? Alternatively, he could continue raiding while homebound and perhaps engage a weak escort to capture a convoy. Following careful deliberation, Captain Langsdorff wrote an explicit statement in his log dated 26 November. He referred to a change in tactics. Mechanical wear and tear had jeopardized *Graf Spee's* raider cruise. Homebound to Germany, he would continue commerce raiding. However, if chance permitted, he would engage a weaker escort to further the cause. Langsdorff found no discord to his standing orders in attacking a weak escort - ***to further the principal task.***

At this time, Langsdorff fatally believed that *Graf Spee's* armor could absorb an 8-inch shell without serious consequences. In his log he wrote: If an opportunity arose, *Spee* would close quickly and attack the escort. Using the pocket battleship's 11-inch guns against an 8-inch-gunned cruiser we can expect success without major damage. The previous evening - 25 November - the captain had advised his officers of his change in tactics. They greeted the news with pleasure, especially Commander Ascher the gunnery officer.

On 29 November, *Altmark* and *Graf Spee* resumed their separate ways. Three days later - 2 December - *Spee* sighted smoke on the horizon. A red funneled liner tried to run from the German warship. *Spee* fired an 11-inch shell from afar that splashed into the sea. It was too close for comfort and SS *Doric Star* stopped to accept her fate. Meanwhile, her wireless operator sent out her situation: *'Surface raider attack at 19°15'S/5°5'E.'*

Early next morning, *Graf Spee* forced another freighter to stop. Despite machine-gun fire that wounded three young British sailors, MV *Tairoa* signaled her position: *'21°38'S/3°13'W Scheer [sic]'* Captain Langsdorff now had eight prizes on his belt but the enemy knew his position.

Still running westward, he decided to steer for Santos Bay, Brazil. Single merchants following the coastal waters might cross the huge bay to save time. When sailing beyond the three-mile limit they were fair game. If nothing developed, he would steer south and show his flag, then turn northward to pass through the 'narrows' and head for home.

Graf Spee met *Altmark* on 6 December at 24°17'S/19°45'W. Langsdorff handed over his latest prisoners to the supply ship. Captain Dau complained that *Altmark* did not have suitable space for prisoners. *Graf Spee* then took twenty-six British captains, engineers and other officers on board to return to Germany. The three wounded lads from *Tairoa* continued receiving treatment in *Spee's* hospital.

Continuing westward, *Graf Spee* refueled underway from *Altmark* and they agreed on a future schedule. At 08:00 on 7 December, the ships parted company to resume operations. Shrill alarm signals at 17:45 sent *Spee's* crew scurrying to their action stations: *'Smoke on the Horizon' at 25°1'S/27°50'W.'* A prize crew soon boarded SS *Streonshalh* before she could use her wireless. They searched her thoroughly.

Captain J.J. Robinson later claimed he had eliminated all secret documents. Following admiralty procedure, he dumped two weighted bags overboard. But *Graf Spee's* prize crew found papers floating close to the freighter that showed her route from Montevideo. Also, the searchers in the ship scooped up Buenos Aires newspapers that reported ship movements.

The Buenos Aires Herald wrote that *Highland Monarch*, a large British mail boat, would sail out on 5 December. Five days later, on 10 December, the liner *Andalusia Star* would follow. Coincidentally, a wireless signal from Berlin described four merchant ships preparing to leave the Plate on 5 December. This signal named the ships and reported their tonnage - *Highland Monarch* (14,000BRT), *Marconi* (7,400BRT), *Ashbury* (3,901BRT) and *Southgate* (4,862BRT). Captain Langsdorff faced a tremendous incentive to change his planned route.

Writing in his log, the captain reasoned that *Highland Monarch* and *Andalusia* would not join a convoy. They could better use their higher speed traveling solo. However, the British might convoy the other freighters, with a light escort, to start them toward their final destination.

Langsdorff decided to execute a search pattern where he believed the ships and escort might separate. A large liner or a small convoy would greatly augment his tally. Disastrously, the Arado float plane had not operated since 2 December. During the cruise, sea water damage on the air-cooled engine had required innumerable repairs. Despite ingenious efforts from the mechanics, the often-repaired engine had finally died. *Spee* must depend mainly on the lookouts scanning the horizon from the foretop to avoid danger or find targets.

CHAPTER 14:

The Battle of the River Plate.

Dawn Action Stations stood down at 05:40 13 December. Following an hour of tough drill, Commodore Harwood's three cruisers reverted to third degree of readiness while sailing in line. Lt-Cmdr. R.B. Jennings, the gunnery officer and executive officer on HMS *Exeter*, thankfully went below. Jennings had stood the 00:01 - 04:00 middle watch before shaving and going directly to dawn action stations. Jennings lost his well-earned sleep when 'beat to quarters' suddenly sounded - calling all hands to battle stations. Gunnery officer Jennings quickly made his way to the director control tower (DCT) to join in making naval history.

About 06:14, Leading Signalman Bill Swanston on HMS *Ajax* had sighted light brown smoke on the horizon. The smoke suggested a freighter heading toward the Plate. Commodore Harwood ordered *Exeter* to investigate. As *Exeter* closed the distance, she recognized a pocket battleship. Suddenly, a cloud of black smoke broke out of the German's funnel as she cranked up speed to attack the cruiser. Commodore Harwood's division smartly swung into their well-rehearsed battle plan. *Ajax* and *Achilles* swept away from *Exeter* to place the German warship between themselves and the 8-inch cruiser.

A terse wireless signal at 06:34 (08:34 GMT)from a position 250 miles off Uruguay reached the Admiralty: *'IMMEDIATE: One pocket battle-ship 034 deg.south/049 deg.west-course 275 degree. Signed CSAD.'*[Commodore South American Division]

Immediately, Operations advised Admiral Pound who passed the electrifying news to Winston Churchill. Both men hurried to the War Room. A few minutes later, another signal at 06:46 (08:46 GMT), advised: *'Am engaging one pocket battle–ship.* **Exeter, Achilles** *in company.'* Commodore Harwood was sailing into battle on his own terms.

Churchill reacted with shock. In his mind Force 'G' could not handle a pocket battleship. Harwood should be shadowing the German. 'Get him out of there' Churchill muttered. 'We can't have a second Coronel.' But round one had already begun. Harwood's tactics must prevail.

Exeter opened fire at 06:20. Lt-Cmdr. Jennings saw his first salvoes straddle *Graf Spee* from 18,700 yards. Then two 11-inch shells wrecked *Exeter's* wheelhouse and destroyed turret 'B'. Momentarily out of control, the cruiser swung to starboard. Torpedo officer Lt-Cmdr. C.J.Smith called into a buckled voice tube to the after steering position for a change of course. *Exeter* swung to port. At 06:32 Smith released his three starboard torpedoes.

Captain bell quickly regained control, with a manual line of sailors relaying instructions to the after steering position. *Graf Spee* had begun a sweeping port-side turn to avoid the torpedoes and run parallel with *Exeter*. About this time Jenning's gun crew landed an 8-inch shell amidships on the starboard side of the pocket battleship. This crucial shell smashed an anti aircraft gun shield, pierced two decks and burst aft of the funnel.

Exeter continued to fight gamely, landing two more 8-inch shells on *Spee's* port side. Then she took a pair of 11-inch hits and retired behind a huge smoke screen. When she reappeared at 07:00, she caught the full effect of *Spee's* 11-inch salvoes. In quick time, flames covered the cruiser and licked high into the sky beyond her masts. She took a heavy list to starboard and appeared doomed. At this critical moment, the German captain switched his main guns onto *Ajax* and *Achilles*. They were closing his starboard side at maximum speed.

Working incredibly quickly, the enemy gunners plastered the pocket battle ship with 6-inch shells at near range. As the battle raged on, *Spee* and the two light cruisers swerved back and forth at high speed to avoid hits. Commodore Harwood had seized the initiative and intended to keep it. Relentlessly he pressed his attack until *Ajax* reported an ammunition shortage. Harwood then decided to retreat beyond the enemy's gun range and bide his time to renew the attack.

Surprisingly, the pocket battle ship also broke off, heading westward at full speed while trailing heavy smoke in her wake. Although peppered with 6-inch hits, *Graf Spee* did not show any major damage.

While the cannon roared and the warships engaged in deadly combat, the Admiralty awaited further news. Wireless antenna damage had left a gap in field reports of the action. Still, the royal navy had found the object of their extensive search. The pocket battleship must not escape.

Then bad news arrived from Harwood. At 07:22 (09:22GMT) he signaled: *'Immediate: HMS* **Ajax,** *HMS* **Achilles,** *HMS* **Exeter** *have been heavily engaged. Have withdrawn from daylight close action owing to shortage of ammunition. HMS* **Exeter** *hauling away due damage, two turrets out of action in HMS* **Ajax.** *Pocket battleship has undoubtedly been hit. I am shadowing.'*

Commodore Harwood's two cruisers now followed *Graf Spee* at a safe distance with *Achilles* off the starboard beam and *Ajax* to port. About 11:00 Captain Bell signaled his situation from *Exeter*. Although badly flooded, the ship was stable and making 18 knots. With all but one gun silenced and sixty men killed, Captain 'Hooky' Bell requested further orders. Commodore 'Bobby' Harwood sent *Exeter* to the Falklands.

Harwood's signal to the Admiralty at 11:17 (13.17 GMT) filled the details: *'Most immediate: Position, course and speed of pocket battleship 034 deg. 44' south/051 deg. 40' west - 260 degrees 22 knots, using call sign DTGS. HMS* **Ajax** *and HMS* **Achilles** *shadowing. HMS* **Exeter** *very badly damaged. One gun in local control remains in action. Speed reduced, maximum 18 knots. Have directed her to proceed to the Falkland Islands. Aircraft reports twenty-five to thirty hits obtained on pocket battleship but he still has high speed.'*

In Freetown, Vice Admiral Lyon had appraised the situation. He ordered *Neptune* to head for Rio de Janeiro, take on fuel and go to the Plate. Lyon also signaled *Cumberland* to sail out and contact Harwood's force. Fortunately, Captain Fallowfield had overheard radio exchanges from the battle and anticipated his orders. HMS *Cumberland* was already steaming at full speed for the River Plate.

Meanwhile, Force 'K'(*Ark Royal* and *Renown*), was running low on fuel. D'Oyly Lyon signaled Rear Admiral Wells to meet with *Neptune* and all ships refuel at Freetown - the nearest British fueling station. The Admiralty immediately countermanded Lyon's instructions: Force 'K' should refuel at a South American port. Admiral Pound surmised that the Foreign Office could arrange fueling facilities at Bahia Blanca, Argentina or Rio de Janeiro. Which neutral port did the task force prefer? Lyon signaled Force 'K' to fuel at Rio de Janeiro and head for the River Plate.

Urgent telegrams from staff in the British embassy at Montevideo completed the picture. First they advised that a pocket battleship had engaged two cruisers fifteen miles from *Punta del Este*. Later with a 'most immediate' heading, they added that a German pocket battleship had anchored in Montevideo roads at 23:50 on 13 December. Finally, they identified *Admiral Graf Spee* anchored in Montevideo harbor.

Responsibility for holding the pocket battleship under siege now fell solely on Commodore Harwood's two 6-inch-gun cruisers. *Cumberland* would not get to the Plate until late evening next day - 14 December. *Renown* and *Ark Royal* must sail one thousand sea-miles after refueling in Rio de Janeiro on 17 December. Two 8-inch-gunned cruisers were speeding to the Plate but HMS *Dorsetshire* would not arrive until 21 December and HMS *Shropshire* two days later. Could Harwood's cruisers stop *Graf Spee* if she tried to escape?

Murphy's Law.

Chapter 15:
Graf Spee's Hidden Damage.

In the dawning light of 13 December, *Admiral Graf Spee*'s crew suddenly scented action. Before the change of watch at 06:00, lookouts reported mast tips on the horizon. Officer of the watch Commander Wattenberg had replaced Lieutenant Rasenack on the bridge: they were readying to change course in their search pattern. Wattenberg reported the sighting to Captain Langsdorff: four mast tips had appeared, then two and now they had disappeared. Langsdorff ordered the ship to stay on present course and hurried from his cabin to the bridge. Had providence handed him a convoy?

Within minutes the lookouts aloft identified HMS *Exeter* in company with two destroyers. Langsdorff assumed the 8-inch-gun cruiser was covering a convoy. He ordered the pocket battleship to 'action stations' and called for full speed to attack *Exeter*. The distance closed rapidly. *Spee's* lookouts now labeled the two 'destroyers' as light cruisers - *Ajax* and *Achilles*. Langsdorff had stumbled into a deadly battle situation beyond his control. *Graf Spee* lacked the speed to chase or escape from these cruisers.

Exeter quickly mounted speed while converging on *Graf Spee*. At 06:17 *Spee* opened fire with her 11-inch guns, but a magnetic relay problem in the forward turret delayed full broadside action. Mechanics quickly overcame this hindrance *Spee* soon straddled *Exeter*, using both turrets, then hit her with horrendous consequences. Still, *Exeter* landed an 8-inch shell on *Spee's* starboard side, as Langsdorff swung his ship violently to port.

At 07:00 *Exeter* emerged from a huge smoke screen. Flames engulfed the cruiser beyond the height of her masts and she listed heavily to port. Captain Langsdorff had a clear view of his victim - he could finish her off with a continued salvo. Lieutenant Diggins, sharing the unprotected space on the foretop with the Captain, mentioned they should watch their ammunition. Langsdorff gazed a long moment at the blazing cruiser - she had nothing left. Then he switched his main guns onto the light cruisers that raced toward his ship.

Soon a furious rain of six-inch shells fell on the pocket battleship. During the action a shell blast knocked Captain Langsdorff senseless. Lieutenant Diggins, close by the captain, had his uniform singed but immediately reported: 'the captain is down'. The Executive Officer, Junior Captain Kay, promptly appeared at the hatch of the foretop.

However, Langsdorff quickly recovered and continued to fight the battle. Suddenly, the two light cruisers withdrew to a safe distance and shadowed while *Spee* continued westward. Langsdorff then made a quick personal check of his damaged sections. They reported unexpected weaknesses in his ship. *Graf Spee's* armor protection - touted to shrug off 8-inch shells - was a fallacy. *Exeter's* three 8-inch hits ran through the armor easily. About 06:38, an 8-inch hit penetrated two decks then exploded in *Spee's* funnel area. Lamentably, *Graf Spee* had received crippling hidden damage.

Spee's main engines used diesel fuel (*treibōl*) stored in bunkers around the hull. The raw refinery diesel needed treatment before feeding the engines. A separating system routinely pre cleaned the fuel and deposited it in six ready tanks, situated close to the engines. The fuel separators used high-pressure steam to function. Two auxiliary boilers and a network of valves and tubes generated the steam. The *Hilfskesselraum* (boiler-room) that produced the steam lay between decks, aft of the funnel. Unfortunately, the *Hilfskesselraum* lay above the armored deck. *Exeter's* early 8-inch hit had wrecked the boiler-room - in effect shutting down the separating system.

Chief Engineer Commander Klepp advised the captain they could not repair the damage at sea. Klepp estimated the ship had about sixteen hours of running time, using pre cleaned fuel from the ready tanks. They could not replace the rapidly depleting fuel.[1]

Langsdorff recognized that *Graf Spee* must go into port for repairs. Montevideo was the nearest neutral port. The Captain signaled his situation to SKL: *engaged three cruisers; Exeter disabled; Spee major damage; intend going into Montevideo - speed 23 knots; possibly entrapped; thirty-six dead.* Several hours later Berlin confirmed Langsdorff's decision with a one word reply, *Einverstanden* (acknowledged).

Graf Spee continued westward and the Uruguayan coast came into view. She had fired a few 11-inch volleys to keep the cruisers at a safe distance. Then *Spee* lookouts reported torpedo tracks approaching. Langsdorff immediately changed course to avoid the danger. Although the Captain reported a submarine attack, he later considered it a false alarm.

As they filed past *Punta del Este* into the River Plate Estuary, a small Uruguayan cruiser - *Uruguay* - approached the warships. *Achilles* then steamed inside the three-mile limit coastward of *Isla de Lobos*, to stymie any chance of *Spee* reversing course around the outcrop. As dusk fell, *Achilles* fired three eight-gun salvoes from a shadowed position against the coast. *Spee* responded with single-shot volleys from her rear turret and chased *Achilles* out of range.

Finally, *Graf Spee* slipped slowly into the roads at Montevideo. The Second Navigating Officer, Commander Höpfner, had merchant ship experience in the Plate Estuary before the war. Extremely shallow water and undulating underwater sand bars caused hazardous navigational problems. However, Höpfner guided *Spee* into the harbor at 23:00 13 December - without the help of local pilots.

Captain Langsdorff meditated long and deeply over his initial battle report to Berlin. He fully recognized the military and political conundrum that confronted him. *Spee's* battle experience denied the theory that a pocket battleship could speed away from a heavier warship and outgun a cruiser. Three months at sea had exposed flaws in the diesel engine technology. Also, *Graf Spee's* armor protection had proved inadequate. Fast cruisers with 8-inch guns could outrun and maim a pocket battleship. Incredibly, a design oversight had left the fuel separation system vulnerable to chance hits. If this deficiency leaked out, ridicule would fall on the navy. Catcalls from the enemy and home grown political criticism could jeopardize Admiral Raeder's surface fleet plans. Captain Langsdorff decided to keep this damning information secret.

Langsdorff sent his report from the German legation in Montevideo at 01:00 15 December. SKL knew about the deteriorating engines from earlier reports. The Captain's battle report stated that shells had pierced the armor belt and torn the armored deck. He specified battle damage involving the high pressure steam system and highlighted the galleys to confuse any interception of the message. But he avoided any mention of the separators. Langsdorff clearly declared they could not repair the damage on board nor break out to the open sea. The captain advised

Berlin that the ship entered Montevideo harbor without pilot assistance. Captain Langsdorff now faced a unique military and political situation whose resolution would echo around the globe.

CHAPTER 16:

Montevideo, Uruguay.

In 1939, Montevideo bustled with commercial activity. The prosperous South American sea–port shipped agricultural products around the world. News about the sea battle off the coast on 13 December spread like a brush fire. Captain Fuentes, commanding the national warship *Uruguay*, signaled a report to his superior officer - the navy inspector general. Vice Admiral Schroeder in turn advised the minister of defense - General Campos - who briefed the president of the republic. President Baldomir listened attentively to General Campos's report of the *Graf Spee* situation. Baldomir, did not welcome any involvement in the European war. Uruguay must remain neutral. The president instructed General Campos to coordinate with Dr. Guani, the foreign minister.

On winning the national election in 1938, General Baldomir had recalled Doctor Alberto Guani from London to become minister of exterior relations. Guani, a past president of the League of Nations, had spent twenty years of his political career in Europe. The international community highly esteemed the Uruguayan politician as a staunch defender of democracy. When representing Uruguay in Paris and in London he had interacted closely with the top politicians of the day. The president now relied on Dr. Guani's expertise to manage any international complications regarding *Graf Spee*. General Campos had no qualms with this tactic. Guani would favor a British position but he must follow the neutral policies prescribed by international law.

At the beginning of the European war, the United States had declared neutrality. On 3 October 1939, twenty-one neutral American republics had convened in Panama. They sought a war-free zone - 300 to 600 miles - off the eastern coast of the American Continent. The United States strongly supported this idea. Great Britain concurred but requested that the United States Navy should police the entire zone. While discussions continued, European maritime nations recognized only the traditional three-mile limit.

Captain Hans Langsdorff had no knowledge of the political situation in Uruguay. Personal experience in Berlin in the mid-thirties had left him with a profound distaste and distrust of all politicians. While attending to his naval duties he would fulfill the high expectations of Admiral Raeder.

Commodore Harwood was equally dedicated to his service. Several years of South American experience gave him insight into Uruguayan conditions. 'Bobby' Harwood knew intimately the waters of the River Plate Estuary and he had many important contacts ashore. Captain McCall, the British naval attaché in Buenos Aires, and Millington-Drake, the political representative in Montevideo, could help Britain's cause immeasurably.

Harwood had signaled McCall that a German pocket battleship might enter the River Plate. Concurrently, a light-house keeper at Punta del Este had alerted Montevideo newspapers of the evolving scenario. Millington-Drake had immediately begun preparations to foil any potential German advantage in Montevideo. Thus, they set the stage for four days of breathless public drama that overshadowed the military undercurrents of the *Graf Spee* incident.

No one knew why Captain Langsdorff had taken his ship into port. In an interview with AP in Montevideo, Saturday 16 December, the captain muddied the waters further. Langsdorff stated that he could not find his supply ship - *Tacoma* [sic] - off Brazil. *Tacoma* now lay a few miles away in Montevideo harbor while his supply ship - *Altmark* - sought to evade discovery in the South Atlantic. The German captain claimed *"he was running low in fuel"* when he ran into the British cruisers. The world's major newspapers published these half-truths internationally. In reality, *Spee* had refueled from *Altmark* on 6 December. She had ample raw fuel in her bunkers. But battle damage had disengaged the fuel separators - leaving 16hrs of pre cleaned fuel in the ready tanks.

In Montevideo, Langsdorff took center stage in the unfolding public drama. The charismatic captain filled the part perfectly. Working with Herr Langmann, the German political minister, they arranged the transfer of seriously wounded crew members to the Uruguayan Military Hospital.

Some sailors had suffered eye injuries similar to those caused by mustard gas. These men received treatment from Dr. Meerhoff, a Uruguayan-German eye specialist at the Pasteur Hospital. Ultimately,

Commander Klepp traced the unusual eye injuries to a chemical used in fighting fires. Ardexin had leaked from containers during the battle and chemical fumes contaminated the men in the vicinity.

Graf Spee carried thirty-six dead sailors on board. President Baldomir humanely granted a request from Herr Langmann to allow a military funeral in Montevideo. On 15 December, three hundred twenty *Spee* sailors accompanied their fallen comrades to the *Cementerio del Norte.* Mounted Uruguayan troops expertly shepherded the procession of hearses, automobiles and buses. Large crowds lined the funeral route with sympathetic silence.

At the cemetery, Herr Langmann and Captain Langsdorff gave short speeches. Langsdorff, in a moving spectacle, slowly laid a handful of earth on each of the thirty-six caskets. An honor guard of *Spee* riflemen fired three volleys to conclude the ceremony. Simultaneously, Langsdorff came to attention and saluted his fallen men. A montage of grief, pride and respect emanated from Captain Langsdorff's farewell salute - forefingers to cap. Langsdorff's imperial navy salute was the reflex of twenty-seven years of naval service.

Many German officials standing near the captain used the Nazi salute in sharp contrast to Langsdorff. Some controversy arose when the international press published a front page photo of the scene. Yet at this time the Nazi salute remained optional in the German navy. In Berlin, Admiral Raeder could clearly appreciate Langsdorff's 'old guard' affiliation.

While Captain Langsdorff wrestled with multiple problems, Commodore Harwood worried about the strategic situation. Why did *Graf Spee* go into port? How long would she stay? With only two 6-inch-gunned cruisers against a pocket battle–ship how could he ensure a successful vigil? *Graf Spee* must not escape!

Commodore Harwood also had a worrisome undertow dragging at his mind. In early October he had taken *Exeter* and *Cumberland* - Force 'G'- on two searches seeking the pocket battleship that sank *Clement.* Shortly afterwards the Admiralty issued an instruction to the hunting groups specifically advising in part: **"Don't lose time searching in open waters if position of enemy unknown."** But two sequential pocket battle-ship attacks against freighters in December persuaded Harwood that the raider was headed his way.

Many years of South American naval experience and every tactical instinct told him to cover the River Plate. Commodore Harwood, had decided to concentrate his three available cruisers into hunting group 'G' to protect this most vulnerable area. However, Harwood did not have a positive position for the raider when he initiated his plan.

Concentrating all his available cruisers into a hunting group stretched his operational guidelines. However, hunting groups habitually used radio silence and no countermanding orders arrived from Freetown nor the Admiralty. Fortunately, Harwood's courageous decision had paid off. Now he must complete the action.

Before the war began, Commodore Harwood had often visited Montevideo with *Exeter*. He loved the South American ambience and consciously built friendly relationships. In 1937, *Exeter* exercised with the Uruguayan corvette *Huracan* (Commander Jose Varela). Their war game scenario placed the small corvette as an enemy ship taking refuge in the harbor. Marine charts showed that Banco Inglés, a massive underwater island of sand, obstructed the mouth of the Estuary. This left a navigable twenty-mile gap separating Banco Inglés and Isla de Flores - a rocky outcropping extending from the shore. Water depths averaging eleven meters in this area ran to twenty meters downstream over a 50-mile distance. Upstream, the uncertain water depths averaged less than ten meters for 25 miles to Montevideo. A three-mile dredged channel led into the harbor. Inbound merchant ships normally used this route with the assistance of local pilots. [1]

Harwood and Varela had viewed two other possible exits for the corvette. One between Banco Inglés and Banco Rouen and another one west of Banco Rouen. Both these routes traversed uncertain water depths - under nine meters.

Now, Harwood cautiously decided he must guard against all three possibilities. At 23:50 on 13 December, Harwood ordered a patrol along the demarcation line of the River Plate Estuary. *Achilles* would cover from Punta del Este to the southern tail of Banco Inglés. *Ajax* would watch from that point to Cabo San Antonio, Argentina. Each cruiser patrolled about 60 miles.

Happily, HMS *Cumberland* arrived at 22:00 on 14 December to strengthen the British hand. *Cumberland* and the two 6-inch-gunned cruisers gave Harwood a reasonable expectation of success if they brought *Spee* to action. Meanwhile, *HMS Ark Royal, Renown, Neptune, Dorsetshire, Shropshire* and three destroyers were steaming toward the Plate, needing about five days transit time.

Shrouded in heavy morning mist on 15 December, *Ajax* drew 200 tons of fuel from RFA *Olynthus*. *Cumberland* kept watch at visibility distance to the north while the 15,000-ton tanker stood off Banco Rouen. About this time lookouts on *Spee* reported outlines of a heavy warship and an aircraft carrier on the horizon. This 'sighting' gained credibility when local news headlines reported the imminent arrival of *Ark Royal* and *Renown* in the Plate. Skillful British intelligence agents in Buenos Aires had planted false information. Their clever efforts received help from the ghostly apparitions of the oiler and the cruisers.

Captain H. McCall, the British naval attaché, assumed control of intelligence in Montevideo. Working with Captain Rex Miller, an ex-army intelligence officer, they organized a close inspection of *Graf Spee's* damage. Volunteer British pensioners watching from merchant ships anchored in the harbor set up round-the-clock vigilance on the German warship. Captain Miller thoroughly interrogated sixty-one British ex-prisoners from *Graf Spee* to gain any useful information.

McCall also enlisted the support of the Consular Shipping Advisory Department. This unit was set up on the top floor of the *Bolsa Comercio* building, above the British Consul offices. They had a clear view of the harbor. Captain Hammond headed the group with Commander Johnson running intelligence. A Marconi representative, John Garland, had set up a wireless link between Montevideo and the Falklands in October.

Mr. Eugen Millington-Drake, the British political minister in Montevideo soon entered the limelight. He had wide knowledge of the social-political structure in Montevideo and enjoyed a long time friend-ship with Dr. Guani. Millington-Drake's political expertise enhanced the British effort to deal with the German warship. Still, British intelligence remained unaware of *Spee's* fuel flow damage and her badly deterio-rated engines. The pocket battleship might sail at any moment. Looking to gain time, Harwood suggested a British merchant ship could sail and invoke the 24-hour Hague Convention rule: A belligerent warship must not follow an enemy merchant from port until 24 hours had passed. Millington-Drake easily arranged this with the friendly help of Captain

Daniel, the Houlder Shipping Line agent.

Herr Langmann had requested fourteen days for *Graf Spee* to make repairs. To verify the damage, Uruguayan officials insisted that a technical commission inspect the warship. Early in the evening 15 December, Commander Jose Varela and Lt-Cmdr (Ing.) Fernando Fontana examined *Spee's* damage. To help their task, they received a German copy of the ship's damage report. However, Captain Langsdorff insisted that his engines had not received any *'battle'* damage and would not allow their inspection.

Varela and Fontana reported to General Campos and suggested three days sufficient to provisionally repair the warship. President Baldomir then decreed a 72-hour deadline for *Graf Spee* to leave Montevideo or face internment. *Spee's* time limit would expire at 20:00 Sunday, 17 December.

Captain Langsdorff realized that *Graf Spee* had served a higher purpose than its raider cruise. *Spee's* fire control systems had worked perfectly. The main guns earned high marks in the battle. Although excessive engine vibration had hindered radar operations, this early system did not connect to the guns. However *Spee's* raider and battle experience had uncovered serious flaws that applied to all three pocket battleships. If the enemy captured the ship in salvageable condition, it would initiate a double catastrophe. They would carefully analyze the top secret fire control systems. Furthermore, they could identify the pocket battleships' major faults. *Graf Spee* must not fall into enemy hands in measurable condition.

Commander Ascher had reported heavy warships in the misty estuary. Newspaper headlines from Buenos Aires gave support to Ascher's sighting. Still, no credible source had verified the capital ships' presence. On the other hand, HMS *Cumberland*, carrying eight 8-inch guns, had shown herself in plain view off Montevideo. This cruiser alone posed a critical threat. Coupled with *Ajax* and *Achilles* in the treacherous shallows of the estuary the British cruisers clearly outmatched *Spee*.

Langsdorff had prepared for any eventuality while awaiting instructions from Berlin. Specialists from Buenos Aires helped the ship's artificers to speedily make essential repairs. Nonetheless, clear headed analysis showed that *Spee* could not burst through to deep water against the three cruisers. The shortest route, between Isla de Flores and Banco Inglés meant crossing water depths averaging nine meters for at least twenty-five miles. Then followed another fifty miles from the ten-metre water line to reach twenty meters. *Graf Spee* drew seven meters and her engine cooling system pulled sea water through the keel.Three determined cruisers equipped with torpedoes and potent shellfire would surely score hits. Sea water, shipped through damage, would increase *Spee's* critical draft. The probability of grounding in the shallow waters loomed as a near certainty. Capture of the ship would then make a bloody, heroic battle futile. Shameful though it seemed, scuttling the ship offered the most logical solution.

Captain Langsdorff minutely assessed his situation and sent his carefully considered situation report to Berlin after midnight 15 December:

> *To Naval High Command:*
> *(1)Strategic Position off Montevideo: Besides cruisers, destroyers -* **Ark Royal** *and* **Renown.** *Close blockade at night. Escape into open sea and break through to home waters hopeless.*
> *(2)Propose putting out as far as neutral boundary. If it is possible to fight our way through to Buenos Aires, using remaining ammunition this will be attempted.*
> *(3)If a break through would result in certain destruction of Graf Spee without opportunity of damaging enemy, request decision on whether the ship should be scuttled in spite of insufficient water depth. The River Plate Estuary. Or if internment preferred.*
> *(4)Request response by wireless.*

Langsdorff had given the most serious considerations to duty, honor, fighting spirit and human life. Militarily, he must destroy his ship - at any cost. Would Admiral Raeder understand his situation and concur?

Effective Destruction.

CHAPTER 17

Successful Cover Up.

First news of the sea battle off Uruguay arrived in Berlin Wednesday, 13 December. Naval operations at SKL received Captain Langsdorff's cryptic signal: **Engaged three cruisers, 0617 - *Exeter, Achilles and Ajax* - 34°27′30″S. / 49°55′ W. *Exeter* disabled. *Graf Spee* major damage. Light cruisers shadowing. Intend enter Montevideo - speed 23kn. Possibly entrapped. Thirty-six dead.** Rear Admiral Kurt Fricke, Chief of Operations, immediately advised Admiral Raeder. The navy chiefs sensed that the captain had no choice if he intended to enter Montevideo - *despite possible entrapment.*

SKL turned out all available information about the estuary of the River Plate. Navigational problems immediately jumped out. Massive shoals of fluctuating sand and underwater sand banks posed problems. Langsdorff could not have picked a worse haven. At this stage, Raeder could not identify *Spee*'s major damage. He knew that the diesel engines were deteriorating but *Spee* was making 23 knots. Captain Langsdorff must have good reason - and no other option - to enter Montevideo. Raeder sent an equally cryptic response to Langsdorff: *Acknowledged!*

Operations contacted the foreign office and asked about Uruguay. Telegrams sparked between Berlin and South America. German legations in Montevideo, Buenos Aires and Rio de Janeiro scrambled to aid *Graf Spee*. They reported that neutral Uruguay held strong sympathies with Britain. Captain Langsdorff's battle report from Montevideo sent at 01:18 [local time] 15 December, arrived at 06:18 [local time] in Berlin. A summary of the telegram reads:

To Naval Headquarters: Admiral Graf Spee Command 195. December 14. Searched for convoy... Sighted Exeter at dawn ... Accompanying vessel first believed to be destroyer, later identified as two cruisers Achilles class... Attacked to close to effective range... Enemy divides... at least one cruiser not exposed to fire and tries to close range. Heavy direct hits on Exeter...silencing both front turrets. Direct hits on bridge causing serious fire ... apparently damaging boilers ... Exeter moves off. Light cruisers close the range on Graf Spee at full speed. Aft turret on one light cruiser silenced ... another 28cm direct hit and probably two 10.5cm direct hits. Third cruiser apparently undamaged.

After Exeter has moved off, light cruisers move off to great distance and remain to the N.E. and S.E. To break out to open sea and shake off these two cruisers is obviously impossible. Inspection of direct hits... all galleys, except for admiral's galley, badly damaged. Water entering flour storage endangers bread supply... direct hit in forecastle makes ship unseaworthy for North Atlantic in winter. One shell pierced armor belt ... armored deck torn in one place. 36 killed, 5 seriously wounded 53 slightly injured, 14 of them affected by poison gas.... ship cannot be made seaworthy for break through to the homeland with means on board, decided to go into the River Plate at risk of being shut in there. Because of expected submarine attack...maintained zig-zag course and high speed. At 12 o'clock at night 13-14 of the month entered Montevideo harbor without pilot. (signed)Langsdorff.

British wireless interception was legendary in the First World War. Langsdorff had recognized the enemy might read this message without difficulty. The captain clearly stated his damage but the necessity of breaking off and going into Montevideo remained obscure. Admiral Raeder consulted Vice Admiral Schniewind(Chief of Staff OKM), Rear Admiral Fricke(Chief of Operations)and Captain Wagner(SKL operations). These close and reliable associates had monitored *Spee's* ongoing mission with increasing interest and praise. They closely examined the text of Langsdorff's message.

The Captain advised that 8-inch shells had breached the pocket battleship's main armor. Langsdorff baldly declared his ship unseaworthy - they could not repair the damage at sea. Why did he head his damages with a reference to the galleys? Bread-baking was not a reason to break off action and run ashore. *Spee's* ailing diesels still produced 23 knots. What was Langsdorff trying to say? Did he lose his nerve under battle stress? An unlikely prospect!

The legation in Montevideo sent a telegram (#181) to the foreign office in Berlin. Dated 16 December, it detailed *Spee's* damage situation but omitted any mention of the fuel system or the engines. A German shipwright from Buenos Aires, had recommended 14-days for repairs. Also, the message advised that *Ark Royal and Renown* were due at the Plate and HMS *Cumberland* had shown herself in full view. Otto Langmann and the marine attaché, Captain Niebuhr, signed the message.

Simultaneously, Langsdorff's situation report (#183) from Montevideo arrived at OKM. It reeked of defeatism that alerted Raeder to something unusual. Admiral Raeder again huddled with Schniewind, Fricke and Wagner for a couple of hours to discuss Langsdorff's report. It stated three main points and asked for a wireless message directly to the captain with instructions:

1. The Captain specifically declared that any break through to open sea was **hopeless**.
2. Langsdorff proposed to put out to the neutral boundary. *If possible, he would try to reach Buenos Aires - using remaining ammunition.* This appeared a very ambiguous suggestion.
3. Two positive choices remained: To scuttle in spite of *insufficient water depth* or submit to internment. Langsdorff focused specifically on the Plate Estuary's water depth.

The marine charts at OKM clearly showed the problems facing a warship drawing seven meters. It seemed Langsdorff was suggesting scuttling the ship, using all available explosives. *Graf Spee* represented the prestigious pocket battleship class. If she suffered a drubbing, the enemy would gain a propaganda bonanza. A military and political disaster threatened if she succumbed in the Plate's shallow waters. Even a glorious fight to the end could not compensate for such a situation. Admiral Raeder reviewed his choices with extreme caution. Hitler would never agree to scuttling the ship without a fight. Nor could the navy accept internment.

In Montevideo on Saturday 16 December, Captain Langsdorff revisited his situation. Repairs to *Graf Spee* advanced rapidly. The Italian company Coppolo with help from Siemens in Buenos Aires had provided technical expertise. Everyone in *Spee's* complement labored tirelessly to fix the damage and prepare the ship for combat. Chief

Engineer Commander Klepp assured Langsdorff that the steam system would regain function later in the evening.

However, they had run the diesel engines for almost 2,000hrs. Four months at sea had caused severe engine fatigue. Two auxiliary engines ran continuously to provide electrical power to the main engines and other facilities. They proved the weakest link in the propulsion system. Every foundation support had cracked - causing serious malfunctions in the main engines. Captain Klepp could not guarantee more than 17 knots under present conditions.

Klepp and Langsdorff acknowledged the fatigued state of the engines. They also saw the continuing threat to the ship's fuel flow. *Spee's* high foretop presented a bull's-eye target for enemy gunfire even when the ship was enshrouded in a smoke screen. The crucial *Hilfskesselraum* lay on the second deck, abaft and below the funnel - above the armored deck.

Wireless information from SKL had advised that *Ark Royal and Renown* had left Capetown on 4 December. Commander Ascher reported sighting the capital ships from *Spee*, but in extremely poor visibility. It seemed likely the aircraft carrier and battle cruiser lurked outside the estuary to join the fray.

Regardless, *Cumberland*, seen clearly from shore and two 6-inch cruisers could stop *Graf Spee* in her tracks - without the big ships. HMS *Cumberland*, carried eight 8-inch guns and the other two cruisers each mounted eight 6-inch guns. All three warships had torpedo capability and 32 knots speed with a draft of only six meters. Germane to Langsdorff's analysis, *Spee* had already received crippling damage from a less potent group - on the high seas. During the battle, *Exeter's* 8-inch shells had easily pierced *Spee's* armored belt. Lighter 6-inch shrapnel had penetrated all parts of the ship. Only the main turrets had withstood the cruisers' bombardments. A torpedo hit in the shallow estuary would cause flooding and inevitable grounding.

Langsdorff truly believed in traditional navy honor. He proudly wore an iron cross won while serving in the First World War. Following the humiliating dismantlement of the imperial navy, Admiral Raeder had miraculously reconstituted the *Kriegsmarine*. Raeder had generously approved Langsdorff's request to return to sea duty in 1935. Rescued from a mindless land posting in the ministry of the interior, the newly invigorated naval officer had advanced swiftly. In 1938 he took command of the pocket battleship *Admiral Graf Spee* - one of the most prestigious warships in the *Kriegsmarine*. Admiral Raeder had gained a trustworthy champion in Langsdorff.

The captain understood the admiral's struggle to rebuild the surface fleet. It was a 'sacred cause' springing from First World War criticisms. Langsdorff fully supported Raeder's commitment to honorable conduct in the navy. Every officer must strive to eliminate any residue of the imperial fleet disaster. The German people must have genuine respect and pride for the new *Kriegsmarine*. Battling courageously to the end and going down with the ship was implicit in such naval traditions.

Captain Langsdorff accepted sole responsibility for his current dilemma. Remembering the unselfish sacrifice of Vice Admiral Graf von Spee and his two sons in 1914, he vowed to amend his current situation. Hans Langsdorff would not leave any spurious stain on his ship or the navy.

Meanwhile, in Berlin, Admiral Raeder carefully drafted his answer to Langsdorff's request for instructions. Hitler must approve Raeder's orders. The admiral recognized that the Führer would never approve scuttling without a fight. But Raeder needed to leave the scuttling option open to Langsdorff. Consequently, Admiral Raeder insidiously let Hitler believe that Langsdorff would try to fight the ship to Buenos Aires.

At 13:00 Saturday 16 December, Raeder met Hitler. Only General Jodl and Rear Admiral von Puttkammer joined the meeting. In his preamble to Hitler, Admiral Raeder fudged Langsdorff's clearly stated facts. Langsdorff said: - - - *"propose to put out to neutral boundary."* And, - - - *"insufficient water depth in the Plate Estuary."* Raeder slightly amended these words to give a vastly different impression. In his preamble to Hitler he said: 'The Captain of *Graf Spee* has *proposed a break through to Buenos Aires*. He requests a decision if the prospect is hopeless, whether he should choose internment in Montevideo or scuttle the ship in the *fairly shallow waters* of the La Plata River.' [1]

Hitler cursorily examined and approved Raeder's orders to Langsdorff - he understood that *Graf Spee* would try to break out. The Führer consoled the navy chief that *Spee* might destroy an enemy warship - even in defeat. Raeder's radiogram 1347/16 sent to *Graf Spee* at 1705 [Berlin time] gave Langsdorff his orders:

1. *Attempt by all means to extend time in neutral waters in order to guarantee freedom of action as long as possible.*
2. *With reference to No 2: Agreed. [Put out to neutral boundary. If possible - break-through to B.A.]*
3. *With reference to No.3: No internment in Uruguay. Attempt effective destruction if ship is scuttled.*
    (Signed) Raeder.

Shortly after noon local time on 16 December, Captain Langsdorff received these instructions in Montevideo.

CHAPTER 18

Langsdorff's Lonely Choice.

Baron von Thermann visited Captain Langsdorff aboard *Graf Spee* Saturday morning, 16 December. The German ambassador from Buenos Aires greeted the captain affably. A small square-built man, the ambassador emitted a 'Party' attitude that Langsdorff recognized. They exchanged niceties and von Thermann accepted a cherished oil painting of Graf von Spee that hung in the captain's cabin. Thermann would forward it to OKM in Berlin.

Langsdorff felt uncomfortable in the company of enthusiastic Nazis. He had experienced a similar discomfort with Otto Langmann, the German minister in Montevideo. The captain firmly believed that politicians and parties would come and go but the German navy was the permanent soul of the Nation. However, in the present crisis the foreign office controlled and managed the action. Telegrams from the Legation carried most of the communications between Montevideo and Berlin. Langsdorff had specifically requested a direct wireless signal in answer to his highly charged situation report.

When Captain Langsdorff received Admiral Raeder's radiogram 1347/16, he thankfully noted item three: *With reference to #3; No internment in Uruguay, attempt effective destruction if ship is scuttled.*

Propaganda had shrouded the pocket battleships in an enigmatic fog. They carried secret components and devices such as fire-control, communications and radar systems. If the enemy discounted the pocket battleships only two battle cruisers would carry the main threat of the German navy. Furthermore, *Gneisenau and Scharnhorst* mounted the same 11-inch guns and state-of-the-art fire-control systems as *Graf Spee*. Militarily, the breakdown of the engines must remain in the navy domain.

Politically, the exposure of the fuel flow system must remain secret. British cartoonists and navy opponents in the German hierarchy would have a field day with this titbit of nonsense. Covering up *Spee's* weaknesses carried a top priority. *Graf Spee* must not fall into enemy hands.

Langsdorff noticed that Admiral Raeder had avoided any comment on the Plate Estuary. No doubt OKM had reviewed the special conditions existing in this area. The captain again noted his chief's emphatic imperative - *'effective destruction'* - if scuttling.

Meanwhile, Saturday progressed and the British net closed on *Graf Spee*. Captain Henry McCall, the naval attaché, visited Commodore Harwood aboard *Ajax*. In the morning mist McCall's dicey transfer from a chartered tug enabled the meeting. McCall's network of watchers had provided a full picture of *Spee's* discernible damage. Two days of close examination with high-powered glasses had shown every splinter from the cruisers' shells that had scarred the pocket battleship. McCall had received the damage report from the Uruguayan commission and an 'acquired' copy of the 'classified' German report.

The Uruguayan commission reported twenty-seven holes in the warship. These confirmed the pocket battleship's inferior armor protection. She appeared to carry less overall armor than an 8-inch-gun cruiser. *Cumberland* in company with two 6-inch-gunned cruisers could probably finish the job - albeit with the potential loss of one ship. They could not ignore the power and accuracy of *Spee's* 11-inch guns.

To ensure the German did not sail undetected McCall's men continued 24-hour surveillance. Captain McCall assured Commodore Harwood he would get an alert from ashore when *Spee* sailed. Commander Lloyd Hirst, a naval intelligence officer and long time friend of Harwood, had set up a private yacht - *Achemar* - to watch from offshore. If *Spee* sailed in darkness, the yacht would signal with flares to show her direction. Finally, an American radio commentator, placed in a commanding position above the harbor, would describe tomorrow's events as they unfolded. The BBC would carry and relay this broadcast.

Captain McCall confirmed details of warships coming to Harwood's aid. Sunday 17 December, *Ark Royal and Renown* would arrive at Rio de Janeiro then refuel and head for the Plate. Also speeding toward the Plate from Cape Town, 8-inch-gunned cruisers *Dorsetshire and Shropshire* would arrive on 21 and 23 December respectively. However, if *Graf Spee* came out on cue, Harwood would have to handle her with the cruisers already in place.

Commodore Harwood's calm demeanor masked the concern that gnawed at his nerves. More than seventy brave British sailors had lost their lives in the early phase of the battle. It comforted him to think that his cruisers might manage the German warship. But her 11-inch shells could wreak enormous carnage in the process.

While the warriors and politicians in Montevideo mustered their energies, the international media carried the drama around the world. In Britain, New Zealand and Germany anxious families of the participating crews devoured the latest reports. Associated Press (AP) reported a remarkable interview with Captain Langsdorff in Montevideo. Dated Saturday 16 December, the captain praised the skill and courage of his opponents. Langsdorff mentioned that *Spee* had met the British cruisers when she was running low on fuel.

The world's newspapers credited the German captain with courteous treatment of his prisoners aboard *Graf Spee*. On the upside, Langsdorff's report of *Spee's* fuel shortage may have given the operations' chiefs a hint. Was Langsdorff using the public stage to flag a fuel problem to OKM?

In Berlin, front page photos of Langsdorff saluting at the cemetery and kindly news reports surely caught the eye of Reinhard Heydrich. The sinister head of Nazi counter espionage(SD) carried a personal grudge against Raeder. In earlier years, the C-in-C had drummed Heydrich out of the navy. The chief of the SD would perhaps probe into Langsdorff's personnel file and examine his recent actions. Whose war was this German officer fighting?

Saturday rolled along in Montevideo and Langmann, Millington-Drake, Guani and Campos played their parts. Langmann had arranged to meet Guani at 18:00 in a last attempt to extend the deadline. Herr Langmann failed totally. Even a veiled threat to shell Montevideo did not dissuade the Uruguayan minister. Langmann argued and blustered for more than an hour then left to advise Berlin.

Millington-Drake kept the foreign office in London promptly appraised of developments. The British diplomat met Dr. Guani shortly after Langmann had stormed out of his office. Millington-Drake sensed the latent power of the neutral American nations. Guani had a tremendous influence in these circles.

Meanwhile, late Saturday afternoon Captain Langsdorff met with Captain Niebuhr, Captain Kay and Commander Wattenberg. They had to decide - provisionally - to sail or scuttle. They needed twenty-four hours preparation time if scuttling. Langsdorff had already decided to scuttle the ship and placed the pertinent facts before the senior officers:

Imperative: The enemy must not capture *Graf Spee.*

Situation: Cumberland and two light cruisers waiting on the doorstep - an overpowering force.

Details: Main engine performance seriously below rated power. Vulnerability of Graf Spee's armor to cruisers' armament while unable to maneuver to fully respond. Insufficient water depth in the exit area to allow free movement or normal scuttling. Additional dangers of engine cooling system fouling in trying to reach Buenos Aires. Enemy capital ships at sea, aware of their position.

Unanimously, the officers agreed with Langsdorff. They should scuttle *Graf Spee* using all available explosives to effectively destroy the ship. No sensible alternative remained. An intense discussion developed regarding naval honor in refusing to fight. Langsdorff squashed any objections - he assumed personal responsibility. Still, they must wait for official orders from Berlin while Herr Langmann tried to squeeze more time from the Uruguayans. However, they could begin now to destroy secret papers and documents.

Langsdorff addressed the assembled crew at 19:30. He assured them he did not intend to become target practice for the British cruisers. Although he must wait for final orders from Berlin, he would resolve their dilemma - in some way. The crew cheered their charismatic captain. These young men would march into the flaming jaws of hell if their captain gave the order. But they wondered what kind of miracle he would produce.

At 19:40 16 December, Langsdorff received the final orders from Berlin: *FT 2239/16 As envoy reported impossibility of extending time limit, instructions according to FT 1347/16 Nos. 2 (if possible, a break-out) and 3 (no internment, effective destruction if scuttling) remain in force.* Captain Langsdorff then went ashore to meet Herr Langmann, who was still fuming from his encounter with Dr. Guani. Admiral Raeder had given Langsdorff authority to scuttle the ship. The captain must now **'effectively destroy'** *Graf Spee* and take steps to reduce negative propaganda.

Herr Langmann and Captain Niebuhr 'guided' Captain Langsdorff in composing a letter of protest. Addressed to Langmann and signed by Langsdorff the letter bemoaned the expulsion of *Spee* in unseaworthy condition. Some passages reflected the anger still simmering in Langmann. These claimed the warship had not used any aggressive pressure although carrying hostile capability. [They published this letter in the local press after *Graf Spee* sailed out. This caused an angry backlash in Uruguay. Although Langmann later admitted his involvement in the letter, von Ribbentrop stopped any further press releases.]

Time had run out on Langsdorff. The captain returned to his ship at 05:30 Sunday morning. Haggard and tired he murmured to the senior officers awaiting his return: "We will blow up the ship tonight. Take steps immediately to destroy all secret and sensitive equipment." In a few words he sketched the escape plan they hoped to execute.

Sunday 17 December dawned in Montevideo. A tingling spirit of expectation pulsated through the streets and alleys of the city. A quiet swell sleepily rocked the ships at anchor in the harbor. Huge crowds had already gathered along the vantage spots on the *Rambla* (promenade) to see the action. *Graf Spee* must move out before 20:00 and meet three hungry British cruisers in violent action. Hollywood could not dream up a better script nor cast a more remarkable set of characters. In command of a German battleship, a handsome well-groomed captain. A big, calm, steely-eyed commodore in charge of the British cruisers. Who would win the day?

As the morning brightened a strident American voice crackled through the radio airwaves. Mike Fowler introduced himself and promised to give a blow-by-blow account of the coming spectacle.

On board HMS *Ajax*, newly promoted Rear Admiral Sir Henry Harwood prepared his three cruisers for battle. A signal from the Admiralty Saturday afternoon had enlivened his mood. The message invested Harwood to KCB (Knight Commander of the Bath) and each captain of his three cruisers to CB (Companion of the Bath). Additionally, Harwood had received a battle promotion from Commodore to Rear Admiral effective 13 December - the date of the battle.

These unexpected honors certified Admiralty acceptance of his courageous strategy before and during the battle. Now he must fight the final round. A short letter mailed to his wife Joan revealed the rear-admiral's concern and natural humility. While planning for victory Harwood prayed for a quick end to the drama - without unnecessary bloodshed.

Meanwhile, aboard *Graf Spee*, Langsdorff's men busily smashed all small instruments and blew up special equipment with hand grenades. Nothing of value to the enemy must survive the coming devastation. Captain Langsdorff wrote a tender farewell letter to his wife. Hans asked that Ruth keep his memory alive and pass on his love for his family. Duty was a responsibility he could not ignore.

Shortly after 18:00 a rumbling clatter from the harbor alerted the excited crowds. *Graf Spee*, like a languorous predator stretching its muscles, slowly moved toward the exit channel. Battle flags snapped at her halyards and smoke drifted from her funnel. Thousands of onlookers watched from every high building. Hundreds of thousands more spectators milled together for miles along the sea front.

When *Spee* reached the end of the dredged channel she swung west and dropped anchor. With staring eyes and bated breath the crowd watched and waited. Suddenly, just before 20:00 the eerie silence erupted in a horrendous explosion. Flames and black smoke shot into the air high above *Graf Spee*. Further explosions punctuated the echoing cries of the dying ship. As in a hellish stage-play, a blood-red sunset lit the tragic scene.

Captain Langsdorff and his senior officers had taken a solemn farewell salute aboard *Graf Spee*. They boarded the ship's launch and set a course for Buenos Aires. A Uruguayan warship challenged them and Langsdorff went aboard it. He persuaded the ship's captain that the Germans were legally obeying a Uruguayan expulsion order. The Uruguayans then allowed Langsdorff and his men to go on to Buenos Aires.

Meanwhile, *Tacoma* had sailed in *Spee's* wake. Lying three miles west of the burning warship, two tugs and a barge from Argentina took off *Spee's* escaping crew from the German freighter.

In early morning on 18 December, the three little ships arrived in Buenos Aires roads with sailors overspilling every space. Argentine authorities consulted the conventions. They refused Langsdorff's imaginative request for asylum as 'refugees from a shipwreck'. After several hours of impatient waiting the Germans landed for processing as internees.

Two days of front page headlines covered the end of *Graf Spee*. Some partisan local editions scornfully criticized the German captain. Avoiding a heroic last ditch fight and destroying his magnificent warship did not live up to the courageous traditions of naval warfare.

On Wednesday 20 December, the critics fell silent. Giant headlines reported the suicide of Captain Langsdorff. He had written a letter to Ambassador von Thermann explaining his intent to keep his ship out of enemy hands. Then in the middle of the night Langsdorff lay down on the battle flag of his beloved ship and put a bullet through his head.

Thousands of people lined the streets of Buenos Aires on 21 December to catch a glimpse of the funeral procession. At the German section of *La Chacarita Cemetery* thousands more pressed around the grave site. Captain Kay, *Graf Spee's* executive officer spoke with feeling about his fallen captain. High military and government officials from both sides in the war expressed respect and sympathy, especially Captain Pottinger, whom Langsdorff had 'hosted' as a prisoner on board *Graf Spee*.

HMS Ajax *(Captain C.H.L. Woodhouse) circa 1935*   — Ajax Veterans

HMS Exeter *(Captain F.S. Bell)*   — MEDINA MUSEUM

HMS Achilles *(Captain W.E. Parry)* — Ajax Veterans

HMS Cumberland *(Captain W.H.G. Fallowfield)* — Ajax Veterans

Admiral Graf Spee *(Captain H.W. Langsdorff)* — Medina Museum

Tacoma *(Captain H. Konow)*   — Medina Museum

Altmark *(Captain H. Dau) Lt. F.W.Rasenack in centre* — RASENACK

Arado Sea-plane in Camouflage — RASENACK

Commodore Harwood's Scribbled Calculations   — Harwood Family

Graf Spee main telemeter (Montevideo 1940) — TROCADERO

CHAPTER 19:
Norway: Combined Operations.

During their naval conference 30 December 1939, Admiral Raeder updated Hitler with the Norwegian iron ore concerns. The Führer listened attentively then suddenly demanded a reason why *Graf Spee* did not sink *Exeter* in the Battle of the River Plate. Hitler's pointed question accompanied a caustic reference to the lack of fighting spirit in the big ships. He had angrily scolded the navy chief after *Spee* scuttled without a fight.

As he faced Hitler's wrath, Admiral Raeder's political skills came to his aid. He claimed inability to give a conclusive report without full information. However, he offered a diversionary explanation: von Ribbentrop's Foreign Office could not extend the time in Montevideo to repair the ship. Shallow waters in the River Plate eliminated any possibility of normal scuttling, opening the bottom valves. If Langsdorff could not reach deep waters, the enemy would seize the defenseless ship. Captain Langsdorff had correctly decided to use all available ammunition to effectively scuttle the ship. Hitler huffily listened and repeated his comment that Langsdorff should have sunk *Exeter*.

Raeder had already issued new orders to capital ships. Once engaged, they must fight until the last shot. They should go down with their flags flying - even in defeat. Paradoxically, he had reissued orders to commerce raiders not to engage enemy warships.

During the stormy meeting Raeder stoically ignored Hitler's rough insults. In his pocket lay a letter from Langsdorff's mother. The Captain's wife Ruth and their two children had passed Christmas with grandmother Elizabeth in Düsseldorf. The family anxiously followed the developing crisis from newspapers and radio reports. Two days before Christmas, Ruth received Hans's farewell letter in Düsseldorf - dated 17 December. It gave an insight into Langsdorff's motivation to end his life but dwelt mainly on personal sentiments. On 25 December - Christmas day - Langsdorff's mother wrote a letter to Raeder. She simply asked if the admiral could shed any light on the *Graf Spee* incident.

Despite the massive problems that assailed him, Raeder wrote a personal reply. Quoting his chief of staff, he related briefly the captain's brilliant operations in the South Atlantic and the Indian Ocean. Raeder lavished praise on Captain Langsdorff. 'One of his best officers, fully committed to honorable duty.' Raeder avoided Langsdorff's scuttling of *Graf Spee* but dwelt on his personal respect for the captain. This private response to Frau Langsdorff reveals a natural decency that lived in the navy chief.

Nevertheless, military recognition of Langsdorff ended on 27 December. Busy SKL officials scribbled 'self destruction in his room, 20 December 1939' into his personnel jacket. Then they slammed shut the book and with it Captain Langsdorff's honorable naval career.

Hitler's acerbic query prompted Raeder to fill the gaps left open in the *Spee* incident. Consequently, SKL sent a signal dated 6 January 1940 to Captain Kay. *Graf Spee's* executive officer had settled into an internment role in Buenos Aires. The wire posed four questions :

1. *Why did* **Graf Spee** *not finish off* **Exeter?**
2. *Why did* **Spee** *run into Montevideo?*
3. *What amount of munitions remained after the battle?*
4. *In what condition were the engines before and after the battle?* [1]

Captain Kay replied to SKL's four questions on 14 January 1940.

1. *Only the captain can correctly answer this question.*
   Perhaps:(a) **Exeter** *was beyond sight, covered in smoke. (b) The captain feared other large enemy ships nearby. (C)* **Graf Spee's** *own damage caused a break off.*
2. *After the fight* **Graf Spee** *had severe damage.*
3. *Inventory: Heavy shells 306; medium shells 423; Flak shells 2470; torpedoes six.*
4. *Every auxiliary motor foundation support had cracks before the battle. This dropped the ship's speed. Extensive hidden damage disconnected the separators for fuel and lubricating oil. Sixteen hours of useable fuel after the battle.* [2]

These disastrous facts, 'disconnected separators and *16-hours of useable fuel after the battle,'* never surfaced in any other documents. A seven-page battle report, sent with a courier from Buenos Aires on 17 January 1940, reported the disconnected separators but it failed to mention the drastic consequences or the cause of the damage. Vice Admiral Fischel wrote a 14-page report on 24 April 1940. It covered *Graf Spee's* tactical performance in the battle. Fischel evaded the issue of the ship losing the separator facility. He did remark that *Spee* had lost her most valuable asset - her range in the vast ocean.

Meanwhile, the officers of the *Kriegsmarine* kept all talk or speculation about Langsdorff and his ship to themselves. Admiral Raeder's navy closed ranks on the mysterious behavior of Captain Langsdorff in the River Plate incident.

Admiral Raeder had weighed the Montevideo situation correctly. He instructed Langsdorff to 'effectively destroy' *Graf Spee* to avoid her capture. The captain brilliantly achieved this objective without betraying the true reasons. Raeder now recognized the pocket battleships' weaknesses - main engine fatigue, weak armor and a vulnerable fuel separating system. The C-in-C navy saw that the potency of his capital ships had shrunk dramatically. *Spee's* sister ships, *Admiral Scheer* and *Lützow* were over–classified. Contrary to expectations they could not outpace a battleship nor avoid serious damage from an 8-inch-gun cruiser. Pocket battleships must take extra care in future missions.

In January 1940, *Gneisenau* and *Scharnhorst* were the heaviest ships in the *Kriegsmarine*. *Admiral Scheer* and *Lützow* were next in line. *Bismarck* and *Tirpitz*, 42,300 tons with eight 15-inch guns and 30 knots speed, neared completion. Despite ongoing problems with Göring's Luftwaffe, work progressed on the aircraft carrier *Graf Zeppelin*. Admiral Raeder's earlier fixation on a world class surface fleet had left submarines in a backwater. Rear Admiral Dönitz's prior appeal for submarines - before all else - had received lukewarm attention.

Although he sympathized with Dönitz's practical assessment, Raeder could not cancel the entire Z-Plan in midstream. At this time, no one could predict the duration of the war against Britain and France. Hitler believed a compromise with the allies might open the door to his intended easterly conquests. If time proved this idea false, he had resolved to invade France and the low countries. A swift victory could pressure Britain to the bargaining table.

Raeder disagreed with Hitler's logic. The navy chief anticipated that Britain would remain Germany's main enemy in a long, drawn out war. Successful war against Britain meant cutting off her imports. Raeder's navy must effectively close Britain's sea-lanes. This incredible challenge posed the question: should U-boats or battleships take the lead position in naval production?

This problem rested uniquely in the hands of Admiral Raeder. No one in the navy dared to challenge his authority - only Hitler had more power. Admiral Raeder answered directly to Hitler but falsely believed he could manipulate the Führer in naval matters.

Unable to get additional naval resources, Raeder cancelled two "H" class battleships - whose keels had already been laid down. Some scarce materials could now flow toward U-boat production. Should he also postpone building the aircraft carrier *Graf Zeppelin*? What about the two great battleships nearing completion? Using every current navy resource, should he concentrate on building submarines? But, would Hitler consent to stopping construction of the capital ships? It was not a simple equation.

Admiral Raeder decided, with Hitler's assent, to continue production on the well-advanced battleships. *Bismarck* and *Tirpitz* should join the fleet without delay. Also, one aircraft carrier with applicable aircraft would help the cause immensely. Raeder resolved to continue pressure on Hitler to get extra resources to build the desperately needed submarines.

C-in-C Raeder considered, how could his small navy contribute meaningfully to the war? Surface fleet action must play a prominent part to earn respect in Germany's postwar military hierarchy. This idea burned obsessively in Raeder's mind as it had plagued Grand Admiral Tirpitz and Admiral Scheer in the First World War. Viewing the global battlefield, Raeder pinpointed the importance of Suez to the British cause. He proposed an immediate major offensive to control the Mediterranean. Stamping out British military power in the Middle East might bring her into negotiations.

Surprisingly, Raeder's arch-enemy Göring agreed with Raeder's suggestion. But Hitler would not retreat from his preordained march eastwards. Other than the powerful battleships, he had only a passing interest in the navy. Hitler believed that Germany's future rested in

Lebensraum - eastern land acquisition. His agenda now focused on invading France.

Yet, he had considered Raeder's arguments regarding iron ore transit through Norway. A surprise attack on Norway would divert enemy resources from his coming *Blitzkrieg* against France. Besides, success in Norway would guarantee the vital iron ore route and provide strategic naval bases.

Suddenly, on 17 February 1940, Norway featured in another chapter of the *Graf Spee* saga. HMS *Cossack* (Captain Vian) boarded *Graf Spee's* homebound supply ship *Altmark* in a Norwegian fjord. The British destroyer, with Churchill's blessing, steamed into Norway's neutral waters and recovered British captives held aboard the German vessel.

Hitler reacted angrily and swiftly to the British action. He immediately allocated five divisions under General Nikolas von Falkenhorst, for a surprise attack on Norway. The general answered directly to Hitler and hoped to achieve a 'friendly' occupation. Hitler selected 9 April to strike. Admiral Raeder's navy would transport the troops and cover their landing. Raeder saw the Norway mission as a chance to showcase the *Kriegsmarine*.

Then Russia and Finland signed an armistice on 12 March and naval high command shelved concerns of British landings in Norway. However, Raeder had correctly foreseen that the iron ore route would draw British interest. On 8 April Prime Minister Chamberlain authorized the royal navy to mine Norwegian waters.

Landing German troops on Norwegian soil presented multiple difficulties. The British royal navy controlled the North Sea. Returning to Germany through swarms of British warships risked disastrous losses. The enemy could muster enough naval power to annihilate the whole German fleet. Raeder realized the immense risks involved but believed surprise would carry the day. Total secrecy must cover the operation.

Gneisenau, Scharnhorst and *Hipper* with fourteen destroyers would attack Narvik and Trondheim. Ten destroyers would carry a landing force of two thousand fully equipped mountain troops. Vice Admiral Günther Lütjens commanded these naval forces. *Blücher, Lützow* and three light cruisers would simultaneously attack Oslo. Rear Admiral Oskar Kummetz flew his flag on *Blücher*. Raeder ordered every available submarine to Norway to join in the assault.

Admiral Raeder had planned to send *Lützow* on a raiding mission into the Antarctic. He hoped to draw some British warships away from the Norwegian campaign. Hitler vetoed this idea and demanded that *Lützow* participate in the Norway landings. Raeder then allocated *Lützow* to join the Oslo group and continue to the Antarctic when she completed that mission. Hitler again interceded. *Lützow* must join the main group headed for Narvik. The pocket battleship's mechanics settled the issue when they reported cracks in the ship's engine mountings. Although *Lützow* would still go to Oslo, Raeder postponed the Antarctic mission. However, the admiral bitterly resented the Führer's interference in naval affairs. An ominous rift appeared in Raeder's and Hitler's personal relations.

German troops successfully seized Norway in a surprise attack that began on 9 April. *Gneisenau* and *Scharnhorst* landed troops at Narvik. Both battle cruisers received heavy damage while withdrawing. They engaged HMS *Renown* in a fierce scrimmage. Encountering gale-force winds and zero visibility, the German warships broke off and returned to Wilhelmshaven.

During the initial stage, a spectacular naval action in Narvik added to the legendary history of the royal navy. Captain B.A.W Warburton-Lee led five destroyers of the Second Flotilla into the narrow fjord at *Tranøy*. In early dawn 10 April, they surprised five German destroyers and twenty-three merchant ships in Narvik harbor. Warburton-Lee's force put the destroyers out of action and sank eight freighters. While withdrawing, the flotilla met five more enemy destroyers. They fought through the German screen and sank *Rauenfels*, an ammunition supply ship. HMS *Havoc* emerged unscathed with HMS *Hostile and Hotspur* damaged. But the German warships sank HMS *Hunter* and beached the flagship, HMS *Hardy*. Captain Warburton-Lee lost his life and received a posthumous Victoria Cross for his valiant effort.

Meanwhile, *Hipper* led the attack into Trondheim but HMS *Glowworm* rammed her before she reached the port. Still, the German heavy cruiser fulfilled her mission. She landed her troops and struggled back to Germany.

The Oslo-bound group under Rear Admiral Kummetz, left Kiel in early morning 8 April. His orders were to enter the narrows leading into

Oslo at 05:00 next morning - behind minesweepers.

To arrive at the correct time Kummetz reduced speed to seven knots. Minesweepers took on the assault troops from the cruisers and the group advanced into the narrows. However, Norwegian defenses had spotted the German ships and Kummetz lost the element of surprise. Shore batteries opened up as the big ships entered the narrows. They hammered *Blücher* and destroyed her steering gear. Then two shore-based torpedoes slammed into the heavy cruiser and finished the job. As her magazines exploded *Blücher* drifted against the sheer sides of the fjord and sank.

Lützow, sailing directly astern of *Blücher*, took disabling 11-inch hits on the forward turret. Confined in the narrow space, Captain Thiele retreated in full reverse beyond the range of the shore defenses. The loss of *Blücher* now left Captain Thiele in command. After Luftwaffe dive-bombers had softened up the shore batteries, *Lützow* bombarded Kaholm.

Eventually, Thiele fought through to Oslo and landed the assault troops at midday 10 April. But German airborne troops had already taken the city. Captain Thiele did not linger in Oslo. *Lützow* sailed out in the late evening and hugged the Danish coast toward home. At 02:01 11 April, HMS *Spearfish* struck her with two torpedoes. The pocket battleship instantly lost both propellers. Listing to port and filling with water, she drifted helplessly toward the Danish coast. Thiele desperately signaled Kiel for assistance. Tugs arrived as *Lützow* was gradually sinking. They skillfully hitched up and towed her to Kiel for repairs.

Germany's invasion of Norway proved successful. Admiral Raeder basked in the praises his ships had earned. However, the cost was staggering. *Blücher, Karlsruhe, Königsberg,* ten destroyers, and eight U-boats went to the bottom. *Scharnhorst, Gneisenau, Lützow and Hipper* all suffered serious damage. Months of repair work lay ahead for the surface fleet.

Adding to Raeder's problems, the Norwegian campaign brought a festering U-boat problem into sharp focus. Torpedoes that should have sunk enemy vessels failed to function properly. U-boat ace Günther Prien joined in a protest that neared mutinous levels. Rear Admiral Karl Dönitz spearheaded the complaints and demanded a high-level investigation.

Admiral Raeder could not deflect nor evade the issue. A major investigation revealed remarkable sloppiness in the torpedo inspectorate. They had carelessly approved torpedo pistols and torpedo performance. Courts-martial and severe sentences resulted. New designers soon introduced technical improvements but the situation compelled Raeder to write an explanatory thesis on submarines.

C-in-C *Kriegsmarine* loftily dismissed attacks on the navy's preference of capital ships over submarines in the Z-Plan. Admiral Raeder claimed that political priorities had privileged capital ships over submarines. Raeder aggressively insisted that the navy now close ranks and keep a low profile on any disputes within the service. In future, if he accepted complaints at all, they had to arise from principal officers with personal experience of the alleged faults. Raeder's rules were clear - zero tolerance of abrasive agitators. Admiral Raeder promised Dönitz additional submarines coming on–stream in late 1940 and gave him personal input into the design of future models. A promotion to vice admiral on 1 September 1940, helped calm Dönitz's fury.

Karl Dönitz had joined the imperial navy in 1910 at the age of nineteen. Raised in a Prussian military family, he easily adapted to naval discipline. In 1914 Dönitz served with the naval air arm and advanced to lead a sea–plane squadron. Then he moved to submarines in 1916. Dönitz's U-boat was sunk in the Mediterranean near the end of the First World War. Captured as a prisoner-of-war, the enemy repatriated him in 1919. Dönitz had an extremely practical mind. Throughout his career he accepted new ideas. Astounding submarine successes in the Atlantic advanced him to admiral on 14 March 1942. This eventually led to his replacing Grand Admiral Raeder as C-in-C of the *Kriegsmarine*.

CHAPTER 20

Winston Churchill at the Helm.

Admiral Horatio Nelson set the standard at the Battle of Trafalgar in 1805. Steeped in Nelson's tenacious spirit the royal navy protected the British Empire. Naval officers and ratings, trained to the highest standards, proudly served King and Country. Political control of the navy lay in the hands of the First Lord of the Admiralty while the First Sea Lord managed operations. They headed a vast organization. Layers of admirals, captains and officers formed an ever-changing command structure that ensured continuity without tyranny. However, huge egos, irrational sensibilities and inter-service jealousies often tangled in personal and political imbroglios.

Hitler's legions attacked Poland on 1 September 1939. German bombers and tanks poured thousands of tons of explosives onto the defenders as the armies rapidly advanced. British Prime Minister Chamberlain invited Winston Churchill to No.10 Downing Street. Britain must react to Hitler's aggression and declare war against Nazi Germany. Churchill's wide experience in the First World War demanded his presence in a war cabinet that Chamberlain had drawn up. Two days later at, 11:00, Neville Chamberlain broadcast to the British public and the world a declaration of war against Germany. Later that day he asked Churchill to take a seat in the war cabinet as First Lord of the Admiralty. Churchill eagerly accepted. Urgent signals immediately flashed throughout the Admiralty network: 'Winston is back!'

Many British politicians of the day described Churchill as 'a loose cannon' - 'a warmonger' - 'a renegade.' In 1903 he had abruptly changed his political affiliation from Conservative to Liberal. Fiscal policies from then Conservative leader Joseph Chamberlain, Neville's father, had infuriated Churchill. Soon he returned to the Conservative ranks but found a cool reception. Since 1935, Churchill had persistently warned the government against Germany's rearmament program. Prime Minister Chamberlain had dallied while hoping for a change in Germany's aggressive direction or leadership, now Great Britain faced a tremendous challenge.

Admiral Sir Dudley Pound, the First Sea Lord of the Admiralty, welcomed Churchill to his new post. The navy remembered Churchill's input as first lord in the First World War. No doubt he would again use his commanding presence to direct the navy with hands-on vigor. Churchill's intense 'requests' usually received prompt action.

Fundamental dissensions had diminished in British politics after the declaration of war. Nevertheless, angry comment fell on Admiral Sir Hugh Sinclair's intelligence department (SIS). They had missed early warning of the recent German-Soviet non-aggression Pact. Lord Cadogan, Head of the foreign service, complained that incoming SIS material fell short in reliability. Admiral Sinclair claimed that severe cut backs in funding had reduced his department's efficiency. They had established a new Central Intelligence Bureau in the war office on 15 March but the individual units lacked coordination. However, behind closed doors, Sinclair's Signals Intelligence Unit had clandestinely achieved important gains in signals' interception.

Germany's failure in the First World War to prevent leaks in coded signals led them to develop new systems. In 1928 they introduced a first-stage 'Enigma' machine for army signals. This special typewriter mechanically mixed a message into unsolvable bits. The recipient needed a sister machine to receive and decode the transmission. Marian Rejewski, a Polish technician, designed a machine in 1933 that could de scramble some German codes. Sinclair's SIS collaborated with Rejewski and Colonel Gustav Bertrand of the French secret service. Eventually they fabricated a working sample of a decoding machine, code named 'bomba'. Consequently, British intelligence could read the German army Enigma transmissions when the war in Europe began.

During September, Germany rapidly overran Poland and the war seemed to pause. British aircraft bombed strategic targets in Germany and royal navy warships sank enemy ships on the high seas. U-boats sank ships around Britain and deadly mine fields became a common hazard, but the war seemed to lack urgency. On 1 November, Mr. Chamberlain and Lord Halifax apprized the war cabinet of secret manipulations that might end the war. A powerful group of German military officers had suggested taking Hitler prisoner. If Britain could offer honorable peace conditions, they would install a new government.

However, due to Hitler's tremendous popularity the military government must permit the Führer a public role - temporarily. Churchill bitterly complained that the war cabinet had not known of these negotiations. Furthermore, he refused to believe the conspiracy theory. As the prime minister and foreign secretary organized their response to the conspirators, Churchill tended to other intelligence matters.

SIS chief, Sir Hugh Sinclair died on 4 November from cancer. Sir Hugh left a sealed note proposing that his second in command, Colonel Stewart Menzies, should succeed him. This note cooled a heated power struggle in the intelligence department. Churchill had actively supported Admiral Godfrey, DNI, to replace Sinclair. Anyway, Colonel Menzies, code-named 'C', became head of SIS: he stayed there throughout the war and remained in close communication with Churchill.

Secrecy and intrigue rested comfortably in Churchill's mind set. He urged 'C' to expand and improve signals' interception. Clumsy mechanical coding machines soon evolved into a computerized system - code-named 'Ultra'. Occupying premises in Bletchley Park, near London, Ultra played a vital top secret role in the Second World War. Although German army and air force signals yielded quickly to Ultra technology, navy signals proved more resistant. During the entire war, Churchill kept close private contact with Ultra information.

On 6 November, Lord Halifax visited Churchill regarding a response to the German conspirators. Britain would demand that the Germans remove Hitler before any negotiations started. But Chamberlain's hopes and the conspiracy fell apart on 9 November when German secret agents (SD) quietly kidnaped two British officers in Venlo, Holland. They hustled Major Stevens and Captain Best across the Dutch border into Germany. Reinhard Heydrich, Chief of the German Secret Service (SD) and his assistant Walter Schellenberg had squashed any hope of a conspiracy - genuine or otherwise.

Meanwhile, Churchill had drawn the war cabinet's attention to Norway. Winter freezing conditions would force Germany to ship Swedish iron ore through the neutral nation. The main transit point of Swedish ore going to Germany was Narvik. Admiral Raeder had already raised this vital issue with Hitler.

Intermingled islands and fjords created a channel that let ships sail the length of Norway within neutral waters. Churchill proposed on 19

November, that the navy should mine the Norwegian channel - the Leads - as in the First World War. However, they needed Norway's permission. The war cabinet adamantly refused to violate her neutrality.

Then a new situation developed: Russia suddenly attacked Finland on 30 November. Churchill suggested that Britain might offer aid to Finland via Narvik. However, war with Russia might arise. Anyway, the first lord still believed that mining the Norwegian 'Leads' would help resolve the problem.

In December, British spirits bounded when Commodore Harwood's cruiser division eliminated the *Graf Spee*. Churchill had already opened correspondence with President Roosevelt. Typically, on 7 January he sent the president a full report of the Battle of the River Plate.

Roosevelt responded with appreciation and remarked that perhaps *Spee's* damage was greater than reported.

In Britain, the spectacular ending to the River Plate action had sparked new interest in Germany's pocket battleships. Many innovations on the unconventional warships remained secret. An electronic specialist from the Air Ministry, Bainbridge Bell, had secretly boarded the wrecked ship in January.

Surprisingly, a mutual friend of Millington-Drake, the British minister and Otto Langmann, the German minister had mentioned an unusual proposition. *Señor* Julio Vega Helguera hinted that the Germans might sell the *Graf Spee* wreck to a ship breaker. It seemed that Langmann needed Uruguayan support for *Spee* officers seeking attaché status in South America. Perhaps Vega could broker a deal to sell the wreck and lobby for Langmann's cause in return.

Weeks of secret negotiations passed between the interested parties in Montevideo. Millington-Drake and Julio Vega Helguera finally struck a deal on 23 February 1940. Thomas W.Ward, the British ship-breaking company, secretly purchased the wreck for the British foreign office. *Señor* Vega brokered the transaction, costing £14,000 sterling and received a £2,000 sterling finders' fee. [1]

T.W. Ward arranged to send representatives to evaluate the problems and costs of working the wreck. Langmann complied, specifying that German specialists would remove some technical secrets before the 'salvage' team arrived. Consequently, a team of British 'ship breakers' arrived in Montevideo on 29 March 1940. D.J. Dyall of T.W. Ward accompanied M.K. (Ken) Purvis (Director of Naval Construction). Purvis and Lieutenant Kilroy (torpedo officer from HMS *Vernon)* led the small group that closely examined the wreck.

In April 1940, Ken Purvis submitted a scathing report on *Spee* to the Admiralty: *"We should not imitate this type of ship. Two turrets form a poor armament. An elaborate fire control system cannot overcome this inherent weakness. The displacement of the ship is too small for protection commensurate with the caliber of the guns of possible enemies."* In his summary Purvis declared: *"In effect the ship failed to meet the conditions laid down at the time of the inception of the design. These conditions were that she should be faster than any existing battleship and have an armament sufficiently powerful to destroy any cruiser which she might encounter. Only the test of war could demonstrate whether these conditions had been met. But there is little doubt that until the River Plate action the Germans confidently felt that the intentions of the design had been realized. The elaborations and extreme measures taken to save weight in order to get offensive characteristics into a relatively small ship made the vessel extremely costly."* [2]

Obviously, Purvis's team could not examine the blown up engines nor the fuel flow system - totally submerged in mud and silt. However, they began to dismantle the top hamper of the control tower to ship parts to England. However, a severe storm on 15 April threw the ship violently to starboard and toppled the main telemeter into the water. [Over time, the bulk of the ship slowly disappeared into the muddy shallows.]

On 11 May 1940, Purvis's 'salvage' team shipped a 4.1-inch AA gun and 25 tons of assorted materials out of Montevideo. Lieutenant Kilroy accompanied the materials on SS *Princesa.* They arrived in Britain on 15 June and soon gave up some previously unknown qualities of the pocket battleships. But the engine and fuel problems that plagued *Graf Spee* remained secret. Captain Langsdorff had successfully accomplished his objective - to effectively destroy the ship, and particularly the information that it embodied.

Meanwhile, Norway continued to attract Churchill's interest. The Norwegian government denied permission to mine the 'Leads'. Paradoxically, German submarines had attacked British merchant ships in these 'neutral' waters. Great Britain had now formed an expeditionary force to help Finland defend against Russian aggression. Code named R4, the force comprised 150,000 men plus six-and-a-half squadrons of aircraft. They intended passing through Norwegian and Swedish lands on the mission. The Scandinavians balked and refused to allow transit through their neutral territory.

Suddenly, an international incident on 16 February brought the Norwegian question to a climax. HMS *Cossack* breached Norwegian neutrality and rescued British prisoners held aboard *Altmark - Graf Spee's* homebound supply ship. Norway and the Scandinavian community gravely protested this aggressive action.

Soon afterwards, on 12 March, Finland and Russia signed a peace agreement. This prompted Britain to dismantle its R4 military force. Then Germany suddenly invaded Norway on 9 April - catching Britain unawares.

Prime Minister Chamberlain responded to Hitler's invasion of Norway with two hasty troop landings. One group landed near Trondheim and the other at Harstad, near Narvik. Admiral of the Fleet, Lord Cork and Orrery held overall command of the Narvik venture while army Major General Mackesy commanded the ground forces. Regrettable and foreseeable, they did not work together 'seamlessly'. The landings met fierce German resistance and the primary British target - Narvik - remained in German hands.

Ultimately, Major General Mackesy gained positions north and south of Narvik but could not seize the port. Mackesy then experienced health problems and the Chiefs of Staff replaced him on 28 April with Lt. General Auchinleck.

Specific orders from Oliver Stanley, secretary of state for war, stated Auchinleck must secure a base in northern Norway. The critical purpose - to stop German iron ore shipments from Narvik. Still, the new army commander had to contend with the command structure already in place. Fortunately, Admiral of the Fleet Lord Cork and Orrery found better rapport with Lt. General Auchinleck. Still, some confusion existed between Auchinleck's written tasks and verbal exchanges with General Sir John Dill, vice chief of the imperial general staff. Auchinleck promptly listed a huge requirement of armaments and materials to support his allotted tasks. Due to critical conditions in other theaters the army could not meet his requirements.

Britain's war priorities abruptly switched to mainland Europe on 10 May. Germany had attacked France and the Low Countries. The allies now needed every available resource to meet the challenge. They must evacuate Norway.

British military strategy called for seizure of Narvik as an evacuation point. Afterwards, they intended to destroy the port facilities and the railroad connecting with the Swedish frontier. In a fierce assault on 27 and 28 May, Allied troops seized Narvik. Then they began the evacuation. The last troops left 7 June and Norway surrendered to Germany two days later.

Public opinion in Britain exploded in angry response to the apparently inept operations in Norway. Prime Minister Chamberlain defended his government against a furious barrage in the House of Commons. The prime minister eventually decided to form a national government with ministers from all parties represented. Clement Attlee, leader of the Labor Party, refused to serve under Chamberlain. Consequently, Winston Churchill became prime minister of a national government on 10 May 1940.

Prime Minister Churchill immediately dove headfirst into the daily affairs of the war effort. One of his top priorities aimed at keeping the United States in a friendly mood toward Britain. Churchill recommended that Stewart Menzies ('C') send William Stephenson to the United States. Stephenson, a wealthy Canadian, enjoyed a close friendship with the prime minister.

In New York, Stephenson rented premises on the sixth floor of Rockefeller Center on Fifth Avenue. Under the cover of 'passport control' the British Security Coordination Office (BSC) worked to streamline the flow of goods to Britain. Keeping track of enemy activities in the United States also kept them busy.

Stephenson contacted Colonel William Donovan, a special envoy to President Roosevelt. Bill Stephenson quietly introduced 'Wild Bill' to British intelligence methods. They quickly found common ground that nurtured a friendly American attitude toward Britain.

Bill Donovan spearheaded Churchill's arrangement to exchange fifty old American destroyers for Caribbean naval bases. These destroyers helped greatly in the war against submarines in late 1940. Later, in March 1941 Donovan strongly supported the Lend-Lease Act of March

1941. This let Britain buy great quantities of American war materials on credit extended by the US government.

William Stephenson later gained fame as the British secret agent 'Intrepid' and Donovan laid the cornerstone for the CIA in the United States.

Winston Churchill's ascent to power came at a most perilous time. Hitler's armies soon overwhelmed France and the Low Countries. Retreating British forces evacuated Europe through the Dunkirk beaches. Fears of a German invasion of Britain gathered strength. General Auchinleck, now General Officer Commanding (GOC) Southern Command, braced everyone for action to defend the homeland.

Despite the Norwegian setback, the general had earned trust and respect from all military and civilian levels. But Auchinleck encountered an aggravating wrinkle in his command. Lt. General Bernard Montgomery, a rambunctious, ambitious officer believed in 'going directly to the top'. Montgomery, as V Corps commander, had bypassed normal procedures to upgrade his own unit with outstanding officers. Auchinleck sent him a series of reprimanding letters that Montgomery ignored. The controversy withered with the need to defend the British Isles.

In these desperate times, Prime Minister Churchill took center stage. He rose to heroic public stature with his inspired speeches. Britain's stalwart people became granite hard in their determination to resist and ultimately win the war. A spirit of confidence settled in the civilian population.

At sea the royal navy ensured enough supplies reached the homeland. A constant stream of merchant ships carrying necessities of British life steamed daily through the Suez Canal. Admiral Sir Andrew Cunningham, C-in-C Mediterranean Fleet, provided safe transit.

On 10 June 1940, Italy declared war against Britain. The possibility that Spain would join the Axis added to the Italian threat in the Mediterranean. Then France collapsed on 22 June.

Germany and France assigned a non-belligerent status to the French Mediterranean. Britain's major life line now required extraordinary protection. Winston Churchill focused special attention on the Mediterranean and the Middle East. When Italian troops moved into

Egypt on 13 September, Britain reacted instantly. They rushed scarce arms to General Wavell, C-in-C Middle East, to repel the attack.

Great Britain and her dominions stood alone against the Axis in this early phase of the war. Adolf Hitler called for plans to invade the British Isles. But Admiral Raeder had grimly objected. The *Kriegsmarine* could not support the massive landing unless Germany had control of the air. Göring's Luftwaffe must gain air superiority over the English Channel.

Wave after wave of German aircraft then met British fighter planes in desperate combat. The Battle of Britain peaked on 15 September and Britain persevered. Hitler paused and ultimately shelved his invasion plans. The Luftwaffe would bomb Britain into submission.

Churchill's enthusiasm for signals interception proved invaluable at this time. Ultra interceptions gave priceless information on Germany's line-of-battle and aircraft movements. Prime Minister Churchill guarded Ultra operations with fierce determination. A top secret 'need to know' strategy guided all sharing of Ultra information.

In Berlin, Hitler preened and strutted with confidence. He intended to bypass Britain and attack Russia at the first opportunity. But Germany's ally Mussolini had no knowledge of Hitler's next move.

Thirsting for a share of Germany's military successes, the Duce sent troops into Greece on 28 October. This raised a political conundrum for Hitler. The Führer had concluded important dealings with the Balkan nations - especially Rumania. A German military contingent now protected the huge Rumanian oilfields and aggravated the Soviet Union. Hasty political negotiations calmed the turbulence but Yugoslavia stubbornly refused Hitler's offers. The Führer resolved to smash this insolent nation.

Responding to Italy's invasion, British and colonial troops landed on the Greek mainland. They quickly overcame the Italians and pushed them back. Mussolini had also run into severe difficulties in North Africa: British forces under Wavell's command had mounted an offensive. In mid-December they recaptured Sidi Barrani, close to the Libyan border. Success followed success and Wavell's desert army captured Bardia, Tobruk and Benghazi by the beginning of February.

Hitler had promised military aid to Mussolini. True to his word, he sent front-line units to North Africa. Field Marshal Irwin Rommel soon earned fame leading the *Afrika Korps*. Opening his first major attack on

31 March, he captured Bardia on 13 April and pressed on toward Tobruk.

Meanwhile, early allied successes in Greece collapsed. Well-trained German divisions poured into the area in April. Predictably, Yugoslavia paid the price for defying the Third Reich. Bombers flattened her cities and front-line troops razed her land.

Despite fighting courageously, Britain began evacuations from Greece at the end of April. On 2 May, the last troops left the mainland and retreated to Crete. German airborne troops invaded Crete at the end of May and forced another British withdrawal.

Admiral Sir Andrew Cunningham gave outstanding naval support in these retreats. Cunningham's warships sailed valiantly into land-based aircraft attacks to pick up troops. They sustained high casualties in ships and men but Cunningham refused to abandon the task.

Britain's cause against the German juggernaut looked bleak until Hitler came to the rescue: German armies attacked the Soviet Union on 22 June. Although Hitler's plans had suffered a delay due to the Balkan diversions, he optimistically opened the Russian campaign.

Admiral Raeder and Marshal Göring had argued for a concentrated effort in the Mediterranean to eliminate Britain. But they could not deny the Führer his dream of *Lebensraum*. Perversely, Prime Minister Churchill continued to augment troops and equipment in North Africa. The *Afrika Korps* tangled with the British Eighth Army in epic desert battles. Neither gained a decisive advantage but each earned the other's respect.

Hitler Takes the Tiller.

CHAPTER 21:

Bismarck Sunk: Admiral Raeder's Sunset.

Determined British troops captured Narvik on 28 May. German reinforcements, fighting northward to relieve General Dietl, met fierce resistence. Admiral Raeder suggested a raiding mission off Norway to help the land war. Hitler approved operation *Juno*.

Vice Admiral Wilhelm Marschall had returned from sick leave and resumed command of the battleships. His overall orders for *Juno* called for bombardment of shore installations or hunting commerce at sea. But Admiral Saalwächter, at Naval Group West, amended this loose directive into a specific order: Marschall must penetrate the fjords at Harstad and bombard the allied beachhead. Then a phone-call from SKL suggested Marschall should protect ground forces moving toward General Dietl. To clarify the mission, the vice admiral called directly to Admiral Raeder. After talking to Raeder, Marschall understood he had a choice of objective when at sea.

Gneisenau and *Scharnhorst* sailed out with four destroyers in company on 4 June. *Hipper* joined the group and Marschall held a meeting of his senior officers aboard *Gneisenau*. On 7 June, while cruising several hundred miles west of Harstad, B-Dienst intercepted signals from various allied ships.

The wireless operators could not pinpoint the exact location. However, U-boats confirmed sighting three large convoys including transports, sailing west off Harstad and Tromsö. Although they could not secure Luftwaffe reconnaissance, a casual report from a pilot advised that only one warship remained in Harstad. Marschall sent out his Arado float plane to investigate. The pilot confirmed sighting a heavily escorted westbound convoy. It seemed British forces were evacuating Norway. Vice Admiral Marschall decided to bypass his orders to bombard Harstad and hunt the largest convoy. At 05:00 on 8 June he signaled this intention to Group West.

Shortly afterward they found a Norwegian tanker with a trawler escort. It took only minutes to send both to the bottom. Then *Hipper* sank the P&O liner *Orama* in quick time. When they came across the hospital ship *Atlantis*, they allowed her to go on unmolested.

Admiral Saalwächter's furious reply to Marschall's signal then arrived. The admiral in Group West briskly ordered Marschall to let *Hipper* and the destroyers seek the convoy then go to Trondheim. Saalwächter emphatically reminded Marschall his primary objective remained Harstad.

Now, B-Dienst identified signals coming from a British aircraft carrier. Marschall believed this must take priority over Harstad. He ordered *Hipper* and the destroyers to close Trondheim and led the battleships in search of the aircraft carrier.

They found HMS *Glorious* in company with two destroyers. After a two-hour chase *Gneisenau* sank HMS *Ardent*. A little later, *Scharnhorst* battered HMS *Glorious* into flames. However, the remaining destroyer - HMS *Acasta* - raced out from behind the blazing carrier and suicidally attacked *Scharnhorst*. Running at full speed through a horrendous barrage she loosed three torpedoes. Although well out of normal range and position, one torpedo tore into *Scharnhorst*. The battleship shipped 2500-tons of water and forty-eight men lost their lives. *Scharnhorst* limped into Trondheim for repairs. Meanwhile, *Glorious* went down - taking more than 1,500 men to the bottom.

Vice Admiral Marschall continued raiding with *Gneisenau* from Trondheim while *Scharnhorst* received patch-up repairs. Twice he found convoys that had powerful escort protection. Cautiously, he sneaked away before they sighted his ship.

Scharnhorst finally sailed for Kiel on 20 June, and Marschall took *Gneisenau* on another sortie. HMS *Clyde* (submarine), found the battleship and sent a torpedo crashing into her mid section. *Gneisenau* returned to Trondheim where she remained until 25 July under repair.

On 27 July, Marschall brought *Gneisenau* into Kiel and faced severe criticism from Saalwächter and Raeder. The vice admiral had totally ignored his instructions from Naval Group West. Admiral Raeder derided Marschall's sorties and refused to give him a hearing to defend his actions. Marschall claimed illness and resigned as flag officer of the battle cruisers. Vice Admiral Lütjens again replaced Vice Admiral Marschall.

Meanwhile, *Admiral Scheer* had received extensive modifications and the navy reclassified the pocket battleship to an armored cruiser. Raeder sent her on a long mission into the South Atlantic on 23 October 1940.

Captain Theodore Kranke took *Scheer* through the Denmark Strait and sank the banana boat *Mopan on* 5 November. Then his pre assigned target - convoy HX-84 from Halifax - came over the horizon. Thirty-seven merchant ships with an auxiliary escort set up *Scheer* for an easy victory. Captain Edward Fegen, commanding *Jervis Bay*, ordered the merchant ships to scatter and fearlessly engaged the German warship.

Sitting outside the ex-liner's 6-inch gun range Kranke pelted her with 11-inch shells. *Jervis Bay* held her position and the merchants scrambled away in every direction. *Scheer* soon pounded the auxiliary into flames and sent her to the bottom. Kranke began to chase and destroy the freighters.

Scheer sank five merchant ships and badly damaged another before failing light ended the chaos. A Swedish freighter picked up 65 survivors from the carnage but Captain Fegen went down with his ship. The Admiralty awarded the courageous captain a Victoria Cross. British hunters could not prevent *Scheer* from reaching the South Atlantic where Kranke completed his mission.

Admiral Scheer returned victoriously to Kiel on 1 April 1941. In six months Kranke had sunk seventeen merchants totaling 113,233 tons, and one auxiliary cruiser. Admiral Raeder happily met Kranke at the dock in Kiel and publicly shook hands with all his men. Crowds of spectators cheered the celebration. Raeder smiled with satisfaction - he had successfully proved his 'two pole' war strategy.

While *Scheer* raided in the southern latitudes, *Hipper* went out on two sorties into the HX convoy routes. In December she damaged HMS *Berwick* and a freighter, *Empire Trooper*. Later, on a two-week mission in February, she found a convoy of empty ships without an escort. *Hipper* sank seven ships and damaged two more before entering her new base at Brest on the French Atlantic coast.

Besides *Scheer and Hipper* raiding the shipping lanes, Raeder sent out *Gneisenau and Scharnhorst* on 22 January. Vice Admiral Lütjens had orders to seek and destroy commerce without taking unnecessary risks. The battle cruiser group sank twenty-one merchant ships and captured another - *Polykarb* - before joining *Hipper* in Brest on 23 March.

Winston Churchill understood that the navy needed an energetic response to the big raiders. But spending greater effort to attack them in their ports surpassed chasing them in the vast oceans. Kiel and Brest now lay within range of RAF and Fleet Air Arm aircraft. Soon, a systematic bombing program on these bases caused Admiral Raeder to rethink Norway as a naval base.

Raeder's 'two pole' tactics caused deep concern in Whitehall but Dönitz's busy submarines gave the royal navy nightmares. Between 10 April 1940 and 17 March 1941 the submarines had sunk 2,314,000 tons of shipping.

At this time *Bismarck* had completed trials and Raeder wanted to send her into the North Atlantic. Operation *Rheinübung,* planned for the new moon at the end of April, would see *Bismarck* and *Prinz Eugen* emerge from the Baltic. They planned to meet *Gneisenau* sailing from Brest and raid North Atlantic convoys.

However, a sequence of damage through bombing or accidental mining hits delayed the sortie. *Gneisenau* and *Prinz Eugen* needed repairs while *Scharnhorst* continued work on her troublesome boilers.

Admiral Raeder then invited Vice Admiral Lütjens to Berlin. Raeder asked Lütjens to sail out alone with *Bismarck*. Lütjens balked and suggested waiting until they repaired *Scharnhorst*. Alternatively, he mentioned that *Tirpitz* would soon finish her shakedown trials and join the fleet. Perhaps they could team the two great battleships. The vice admiral feared meeting enemy aircraft carriers: he vehemently opposed a solo *Bismarck* mission.

When Hitler visited Gdynia in mid-May Lütjens expressed his concerns in a private meeting. The Führer listened but did not interfere with the navy chief's plans. Admiral Raeder finally agreed to wait for *Prinz Eugen* to join *Bismarck* in the mission.

Both heavy ships left Gdynia 18 May. In company with a flotilla of smaller vessels they sailed into the North Sea. General Admiral Carls's Naval Group North had planned the details. *Bismarck* anchored in Grimstadfjord while *Prinz Eugen* and the accompanying destroyers refueled in Kalvanes Bay.

Lütjens intended breaking into the North Atlantic through the Denmark Straits rather than the Iceland-Faroes route that Group North preferred. Anyway, enemy agents in Gdynia and vigilant neutrals had warned the British Admiralty about the German warships' movements. The Admiralty dispatched aircraft and cruisers to spot the German battle group. Then they positioned HMS *Hood* and *Prince of Wales* with six destroyers to cover both routes into the North Atlantic. Meanwhile, the remainder of the Home Fleet sailed out, anticipating an engagement with the new German battleship.

On 22 May, Admiral Raeder broke the news to Hitler that *Bismarck* had gone out. The Führer blasted Raeder for hiding a sortie with his largest battleship until four days after she had sailed. In Raeder's own account "the Fuhrer had lively misgivings." This was the final straw in Raeder's relations with Hitler. The dictator decreed that in future he must approve all movements of the big ships - before the fact.

HMS *Suffolk* first sighted *Bismarck* eastward of the Greenland ice-edge. It was 19:22 on 22 May. Captain R.M.Ellis reported his finding to Rear Admiral Wake-Walker, aboard HMS *Norfolk*. The rear admiral relayed the signal to C-in-C Home Fleet, Admiral Sir John Tovey. The hunt was on! Vice Admiral Lütjens knew it from his radar-detection equipment.

HMS *Prince of Wales* sighted the enemy battle group at 05:52 on 24 May. In company with HMS *Hood*, the two British warships opened fire on *Bismarck and Prinz Eugen*. *Bismarck* replied and hit *Hood* with a 15-inch shell that ignited the aft 15-inch magazine. HMS *Hood* exploded into a hellish mountain of burning wreckage - only three sailors survived. But *Bismarck* sprang an oil leak that slowed her speed to 28 knots.

Admiral Lütjens decided to head for St. Nazaire on the French coast. Like a howling pack, in the evening 24 May, the Home Fleet picked up the scent. Lütjens sent *Prinz Eugen* ahead on its own to Brest. At 23:50, a flight of Swordfish torpedo aircraft from HMS *Victorious* attacked *Bismarck*. One torpedo struck the target without causing critical damage. However, vibrations from the warship's defensive action had worsened the oil leak - Lütjens could not better 16 knots. Still, British communications problems and clever German seamanship in foul weather disjointed the hunting group. They lost contact with the prey.

Unfortunately for *Bismarck*, at 10:30 on 26 May, an enemy flying boat found the great battleship steaming toward the French coast. Home

Fleet battleships could not cover the distance in time to prevent the German's escape. However, Vice Admiral Sir James Sommerville's Force 'H' came to the rescue. Steaming northward from Gibraltar, Sommerville dispatched Swordfish aircraft from HMS *Ark Royal* to intercept *Bismarck*. At 19:10 they mounted a successful torpedo attack. *Bismark's* port rudder took a beating and the ship swung out of control. Destroyers from Sommerville's group were racing to the scene.

At 01:00 on 27 May, Captain Philip Vian's Fourth Flotilla attacked the crippled battleship. However, Admiral Lütjens managed to get his ship underway, making 10 knots. In the murky weather at 02:40, he lost the destroyers. But about three hours later, HMS *Maori* again sighted the *Bismarck*. Admiral Tovey's powerful battleships arrived with the morning light.

The previous evening Lütjens had sent a resolute signal to Hitler saying "We will fight to the last." Hitler replied with "Grateful thanks." Raeder sent a signal "Our thoughts are with you." Saalwächter also sent a signal "Best wishes." Sadly, on this day Vice Admiral Lütjens celebrated his 52nd birthday.

At 08:47 HMS *King George V* and *Rodney* opened fire. *Rodney's* 16-inch guns coupled with the flagship's 14-inch bombardment rained on *Bismarck* for almost two hours. Simultaneous torpedo attacks from other units added to the melee.

Bismarck fought ferociously against tremendous odds. Shattered and listing, she remained afloat until Lütjens ordered the sea-cocks opened. At 10:40, the great warship slipped below the surface. Nearly two thousand officers and men, including Admiral Lütjens, Captain Lindemann and Commander Paul Ascher (ex *Graf Spee)* went down with the ship. International media loudly acclaimed the successful action against the *Bismarck*. The news sent new waves of optimism through the British public.

In sharp contrast, a war-winning event slipped silently into place in England. Early in 1941, a group of cryptologists at Bletchley Park broke the German navy enigma code. Ultra could now read the Germans' naval orders almost as quickly as the recipients. When *Lützow* tried to break out into the Atlantic on 12 June, a torpedo-carrying Beaufort pounced on her and struck her port quarter. *Lützow's* engines stopped and she listed to port with the upper part of her main deck level with the sea. Escorting destroyers smartly fastened tow lines and prevented her from sinking. They towed *Lützow* back to Stavanger.

Admiral Scheer left Swinemünde on 4 September after another major refit. Captain Meendsen-Bohlken took her for sea trials in the Kattegat. The allies immediately picked up the scent and dispatched four B-17 Flying Fortresses on 8 September to attack the warship. Luckily, Luftwaffe fighters intercepted the bombers and saved the day. The German captain took his ship back to port to await further orders.

Meanwhile, Germany had suddenly attacked the Soviet Union on 22 June. A new phase of naval warfare beckoned. British convoys supporting the Soviets would pass through the seas North of Norway. In past meetings, Hitler had often expressed concern of an allied invasion coming from this direction.

Admiral Raeder went to Rastenburg, East Prussia on 17 September for the monthly Führer conference. Hitler vented his anger on the navy chief. He ranted about the battleships as "good for nothing.". . . "They should protect the Norwegian coast or perhaps be dismantled and the guns used in coastal defense.". . . "U-boats can look after the Atlantic." Hitler aimed to emasculate the navy chief and take personal control of the big ships.

Admiral Raeder tried to sell the idea of a powerful sortie into the North Atlantic. He wanted to use *Tirpitz and Hipper* sailing from the Baltic to join with *Scharnhorst, Gneisenau and Prinz Eugen* coming out of Brest. They would form a strong battle group to raid the shipping lanes. Hitler vetoed the idea. In fact he vetoed all sorties into the Atlantic. Raeder hoped his future relationship with Hitler might improve. This did not happen.

At the Führer conference 13 November, Raeder reported good progress of repairs on *Scharnhorst and Gneisenau*. When they repaired damage sustained from enemy bombing, he proposed raiding Gibraltar convoys in February. Hitler vetoed the suggestion out of hand. The admiral then asked permission to send *Admiral Scheer* on another sortie into the Indian Ocean. Hitler instantly refused.

Admiral Raeder mentioned the increasing vulnerability of the battle cruisers based in Brest. He recommended they should move to home ports in Germany. Hitler perked up and asked how they might route the ships. Raeder suggested that *Prinz Eugen* could slip through the English Channel and the battle cruisers through the Denmark Strait. Hitler let the idea germinate in his mind. This augured future problems for the navy chief.

CHAPTER 22:
Battleships Scrapped: Raeder Resigns.

British bombers began battering Brest in January 1942. Prime Minister Churchill wanted the battle cruiser base shut down. Admiral Raeder decided to move his warships to safety and Hitler agreed. The Atlantic base had become untenable for *Scharnhorst* and *Gneisenau*. However, Raeder considered that escaping through the English Channel carried too much risk. Supreme Commander Hitler refused to accept the navy chief's opinion. Finally, unable to dissuade the Führer, Raeder washed his hands of the proposed channel routing. Hitler persisted; he reasoned that the British could not react quickly enough to prevent the warships' escape.

Scharnhorst, Gneisenau and *Prinz Eugen* under the command of Vice Admiral Ciliax left Brest at 21:00 on 11 February. Destroyers, motor torpedo boats and aircraft lent support. Brazenly, the small German battle fleet stormed through the waiting British defenses. They reached home bases on 13 February at Wilhelmshaven and Brunsbuttel. Only mines, in the last leg of the trip, caused significant damage to the battle cruisers. Hitler beamed with satisfaction. Although both heavy ships received serious damage, they had accomplished an outstanding propaganda success. Adolf Hitler had called the successful play.

Understandably, Admiral Raeder did not share Hitler's delight. Repair crews estimated that *Gneisenau and Scharnhorst* needed six months to repair. The warships made their way to Kiel but British bombers had extended their range - Kiel now came under the same threat as Brest.

At this time, frequent North Atlantic convoys to Russia caused Hitler growing concern. German aircraft reconnaissance on 5 March reported PQ-12 steaming south of Jan Mayen Island. Evidently, only corvettes and destroyers escorted the freighters. Vice Admiral Ciliax, now commanding Battle Group 1, received orders to sortie with *Tirpitz* and three destroyers.

Admiral Sir John Tovey, sailing with the British Home Fleet 200 miles south of the convoy, monitored the situation. Ultra intercepts informed Tovey of *Tirpitz's* position and the Home Fleet moved to intercept. However, Ciliax could not find the British convoy and despite Ultra assistance Tovey could not immediately spot *Tirpitz*.

Early in the morning 8 March, a plane from HMS *Victorious* sighted the German battleship. In company with three destroyers she steamed south easterly, 80 miles west of Vestfjord. Tovey sent out Albacore torpedo-planes to attack the great warship. However, *Tirpitz's* ferocious defensive fire coupled with fierce headwinds, thwarted the attack. Lacking air cover from the Luftwaffe, *Tirpitz* ran into Vestfjord en route to Foettenfjord. Admiral Raeder took this instance to broach to Hitler the matter of lukewarm Luftwaffe support for his warships.

During the discussion he convinced the Führer to reinstate construction on the aircraft carrier *Graf Zeppelin*. Raeder had proposed that the new aircraft carrier should join a battle group in Norwegian waters. *Tirpitz, Scharnhorst, Lützow, Admiral Scheer* and twelve destroyers would form the group. This idea played into Hitler's obsessive concern that the allies would land an invasion force in Norway. But Raeder's relative success dimmed when fuel-oil shortages hit the navy. A top secret instruction on 28 March suspended all heavy ship operations - because of fuel shortages. Another directive followed a few days later, suspending all surface fleet activities except in a defensive response.

Allied bombers had now expanded operations. They targeted the German installations at Trondheim. Heavy anti-aircraft defenses with effective smokescreen units helped protect the warships. But in Kiel the bombers finished *Gneisenau* - bombs blew the bow section out of the battle cruiser. She received so much damage that the navy towed her to Gdynia, for a complete overhaul. They intended to upgrade her 11-inch guns to 15-inch caliber - but *Gneisenau* never went to sea again.

In an incredible turn around at the May conference, Hitler revised his naval plans. The Führer ordered a total naval offensive to stop the convoys running to Russia. Plus he ordered *Admiral Scheer* on a raiding sortie. Pumped with confidence following his 'successful' channel break, Hitler assumed the role of naval strategist.

Grand Admiral Raeder had lost direct control of his navy, he felt his lifetime's work crumbling beneath his feet. To date - 1942 - the German armies and air forces had carried the main burden of the war. Raeder's surface fleet had served courageously but fell short of a major contribution. By contrast, submarines had sunk enormous tonnages of enemy shipping.

Raeder also sensed the changing pace of the war. Every day the United States juggernaut manufactured more and better war materials. Ever increasing fleets of bombers plastered German production plants and facilities. Germany could not withstand the free-flowing output of the American war economy for long. Admiral Raeder desperately sought to feature the high quality and competence of Germany's surface warships. They must attack and frustrate the Russian convoys.

Flying into Trondheim in May, Raeder met Admiral Otto Schniewind, Vice Admiral Kummetz and General Admiral Rolf Carls. Putting their heads together they decided to attack 'with full strength' convoy PQ-17. The British had scheduled this huge convoy to leave Reykjavik at the end of June. Operation *Rosselsprung* would prove the value of the battle fleet.

Meanwhile, in the British camp, Sir Dudley Pound held some concerns about PQ-17. The First Sea Lord had crossed swords with Fleet Commander Admiral Tovey. Admiral Pound wanted all thirty-four ships in PQ-17 to travel together but Admiral Tovey preferred they split the convoy into two segments. Furthermore, the fleet admiral feared Luftwaffe bomber attacks on his escorting warships if they steamed too far eastward.

Sir Dudley suggested that Tovey escort the merchant ships to Bear Island then let them continue to Murmansk independently. Tovey totally disagreed! Admiral Sir Dudley Pound then withdrew into Admiralty policy: the complete convoy would sail and scatter if attacked.

Convey PQ-17, thirty-three merchants and a tanker, left Reykjavik on 27 June. Six destroyers, four corvettes with some armed trawlers and anti-aircraft vessels formed the close escort. Two days later, Tovey's covering force left Scapa Flow: HMS *Duke of York*, USS *Washington*, HMS *Victorious*, two cruisers and fourteen destroyers took station between Iceland and Bear Island. Admiral Tovey had received an Ultra warning that the German battle fleet would attack the convoy.

B-Dienst wireless intercepts on 1 July alerted the Germans that PQ-17 had sailed. Submarine U-255 picked up the scent and shadowed the convoy while transmitting homing signals. Lt-Cmdr. Reches' signals attracted nine fellow U-boats.

Admiral Schniewind's Battle Group 1, *Tirpitz*, *Hipper* and four destroyers, left Trondheim at night 2 July. Next morning at dawn, thick mist caused three destroyers to strike uncharted rocks off Gimsöy. During the forced delay, Schniewind sent a sea-plane to Narvik with orders to contact Kiel on the 'secure' land line. The admiral needed an executive order from Naval Group North to cover his premature sailing. Plus, he required an order to sortie against PQ-17 next morning - 4 July. Schniewind then continued to Altenfjord, leaving the damaged ships behind.

Battle Group 2 with *Lützow and Scheer* under Kummetz's command left Narvik on 2 July. *Lützow* ran aground in thick fog and the damage forced her to withdraw.

Tirpitz, *Hipper*, and the destroyer *Friedrich Ihn* met *Scheer* in Altenfjord at 10:30 on 4 July. Admiral Schniewind strained at the bit to sail out and tackle PQ-17. However, a standing order held his Battle Group fettered. Hitler had placed a restriction on *Tirpitz* - the battleship must not engage in any sortie involving aircraft carriers.

Schniewind's command link passed from Naval Group North (Kiel) to OKM in Berlin. General Admiral Carls in Kiel received Schniewind's request for orders on 3 July. Carls realized that Schniewind had sailed ahead of any executive order in his eagerness to attack the convoy. Therefore, Admiral Carls signaled directly to the flagship to cover Schniewind's premature movement. The general admiral's signal on 3 July read, *"proceed to Altenfjord - request intentions."* Carls then relayed Schniewind's waiting situation to Admiral Raeder in Berlin.

Raeder could not place the Home Fleet's aircraft carrier - HMS *Victorious*. Therefore, he could not seek Hitler's authority to send out *Tirpitz*. Schniewind angrily waited - he could not leave Altenfjord without an executive order from Raeder.

Meanwhile, serious problems had developed in Sir Dudley Pound's domain. A reliable report had placed *Scheer* in Altenfjord on 3 July. Ultra information had added that *Tirpitz* would join her on 4 July. Sir Dudley needed to know the status of *Tirpitz*. Admiral Pound had direct access to the Ultra command post in London. Twice during 4 July, Pound visited Commander Ned Denning, who ran the Operations Intelligence Center

(OIC). Denning told him they had a delay at Bletchley Park in decoding incoming Enigma traffic. They were using emergency measures to hasten the relevant messages.

As time moved on, the Ultra system could not guarantee that *Tirpitz* remained in Altenfjord. Neither submarines in the area nor Norwegian secret agents could confirm the battle group's status. Had they already broken out? Admiral Pound imagined the German battle group rapidly closing on PQ-17.

Lacking contrary information, Sir Dudley made a 'worst scenario' decision: he ordered the convoy to scatter. At 21:11 on 4 July Rear Admiral Hamilton, commander of the cruiser escort, received a signal: *"Most immediate. Cruisers to retire westward at high speed."* Twelve minutes later Commander Jack Brown, commanding the close escort, read his instructions. *"Secret. Immediate. Owing to threat from surface ships, convoy to disperse and proceed to Russian ports."* At 21:36 the First Sea Lord sent a signal to PQ-17: *"Secret: Most immediate: Convoy is to scatter."* Admiral Schniewind, still fuming in Altenfjord, had no knowledge of the British dispersal.

Meanwhile Admiral Raeder in Berlin struggled to piece together confusing information. A Luftwaffe pilot on 3 July reported sighting battleships and cruisers close to the convoy. In fact he had seen Rear Admiral Hamilton's cruisers. A little later U-457 confirmed the Luftwaffe information then changed his mind. Another Luftwaffe pilot, shadowing the convoy, reported seeing two torpedo-carrying planes. These were in fact float plans from USS *Wichita*. Arctic conditions can incredibly distort visibility!

At midnight 4 July, U-457 reported the British cruisers speeding westward. Admiral Carls pressed Raeder to send out the waiting battle group immediately. Still, the grand admiral held off approaching Hitler - Raeder had to account for the British Home Fleet aircraft carrier.

Finally, a reconnaissance aircraft sighted the Home Fleet, including the aircraft carrier *Victorious*. At 06:55 on 5 July they patrolled near Bear Island, at least 800 miles from the convoy. Carls again signaled Raeder who immediately contacted Hitler. Hours later, at 11:30 Hitler gave his affirmation. Raeder signaled the executive order to Carls who relayed it to Schniewind. However, Raeder's orders included many cautions: *"A brief operation with 'partial success' is more important than victory taking too much time."* Schniewind must report at once if enemy aircraft showed up. Also, he must not hesitate to break off: *"On no account give the enemy any chance of success over the nucleus of the fleet."* How could Schniewind raise his group's fighting enthusiasm with these timid directions?

Undaunted, Admiral Schniewind rushed his battle group out of Altenfjord - before receiving official confirmation of his orders. At 15:00 the mighty warships raced through the Barents Sea churning out 25 knots. Two hours into the sortie a Soviet submarine (K-21) fired a full salvo of torpedoes at *Tirpitz*. None came close. A Catalina picked up the scent at 18:00 and HMS *Unshaken* (submarine) also sighted the German battle group. B-Dienst efficiently intercepted and decoded the British signals.

Steaming at full speed, Schniewind's group began to run through debris and wreckage floating on the surface. Submarines and aircraft strikes had already decimated PQ-17. At 21:00 Raeder decided to abort the raid. Carls transmitted the signal to Schniewind at 21:15 *"KR-KR-KR Break Break Break."* En route to home base, *Tirpitz* briefly stood off the North Cape but soon returned to Altenfjord. The battle group then steamed toward Narvik with resentment simmering in every soul.

Sir Dudley Pound's preemptive order to disperse the merchants cost a fearful price. Running without escorts the merchant ships took horrendous punishment from aircraft and submarine attacks. U-boats sank nine ships (56,611 tons) and the Luftwaffe added eight more (40,376 tons). The Germans damaged seven more merchants and sank them later for a further 46,982 tons. Germany lost five aircraft.

Nevertheless, Admiral Raeder stubbornly persisted in his endeavor to keep the surface fleet in action. In the second half of August, *Admiral Scheer* (Captain Meendsen-Bohlken) made a sortie into the Kara Sea. Leaving Narvik on 16 August, she bombarded shore installations at Cape Zhelanija and then sank a Soviet icebreaker. Continuing the mission she bombarded Novy Dikson on 27 August. Heavy shore batteries and armed freighters in port replied with great spirit. Two direct hits sent *Scheer* out of range and back to Narvik. She arrived on 30 August with extensive damage. Operation *Wunderland* had fizzled out quickly.

Time was now taking a toll on *Tirpitz* - she needed a serious refit. Admiral Raeder proposed sending her to Germany for expert work but Hitler refused permission. Consequently, Raeder sent the battleship on

23 October to Foettenfjord where special crews imported from Germany began the rework.

Meanwhile, a good opportunity arose to attack a convoy of empty vessels returning home. Intelligence reported convoy QP-15 leaving Kola Inlet on 17 November. *Hipper* and two destroyers prepared to sail but Raeder cancelled the action: he could not muster aircraft reconnaissance from the Luftwaffe.

A pall of uncertainty hung in the air at the Führer conference on 19 November. Admiral Raeder again bitterly complained about non cooperation from Göring's Luftwaffe. Also, he grumbled about the inconvenient *Tirpitz* refit in Norway and the crushing shortage of fuel oil. Raeder suggested they concentrate all naval energies in attacking the returning QP (empty ship) convoys. These did not have serious escort protection.

News from North Africa did not lighten the mood. The British Eighth Army had broken through Rommel's lines at El Alamein in October. A massive allied invasion force had landed on 8 November in Morocco and Algeria. However, Hitler retained an unremitting obsession to protect Norwegian waters against invasion. The Führer insisted that Raeder assign more light forces to the Northern Zone. Furthermore, he wanted twenty-three U-boats permanently ready for Arctic waters.

Raeder for his part needed more heavy units in Norway. The admiral wanted *Hipper, Prinz Eugen* and *Lützow* to join Schniewind's Battle Group 1. But Hitler would permit only *Lützow* to go north - because she used diesel fuel. Finally, *Lützow* slipped out of Gdynia 10 December 1942 and headed for Altenfjord. *Admiral Scheer* needed major repairs in Germany and Raeder had bargained for *Hipper* to replace *Scheer* in the northern group. In spite of the asphyxiating fuel problem Admiral Raeder hoped for distinguished naval action in the coming months.

Following the devastating losses of PQ-17 the British Admiralty had changed tactics. A large convoy designated JW-51B left Loch Ewe on 14 December. U-boats and aircraft reported a light escort. Hitler approved Raeder's request to attack the convoy. Admiral Raeder assigned the task to Vice Admiral Kummetz's Group 2. *Lützow, Hipper* and three destroyers made up the task force under the code name *Regenbogen..* During the two-hour Arctic day, Oskar Kummetz planned to attack the convoy in a pincer move. *Hipper* and her destroyers would drive the convoy onto *Lützow's* 11-inch guns.

Meanwhile, another convoy, designated JW-51A, arrived in Murmansk on Christmas day and unloaded 100,000 tons of war materials. They had left Loch Ewe on 15 December with two cruisers and nine destroyers providing close escort. HMS *King George V* in company with the cruisers and destroyers of the Home Fleet played a back-up role.

German intelligence knew nothing of this convoy until it arrived, nor did Admiral Raeder. Herr Hitler burst into a fuming rage. The German Sixth Army faced annihilation at Stalingrad. Increasingly bad news arrived in a stream from North Africa. Now this! Hitler railed at Raeder about the useless battleships lying idle in the fjords. Consequently, Kummetz's force sailed from Altenfjord on 30 December primed and determined to catch and punish JW-51B. However, a cautioning signal from Admiral Fricke, Chief of Operations in SKL, reminded Kummetz *"it was undesirable to run risks with the heavy ships."*

Working to plan, at 02:30 on 31 December, Kummetz divided his force into two groups. They spread out and searched for the convoy. *Hipper* made contact at 07:54 but because of low light and poor visibility Kummetz decided to shadow. HMS *Obdurate* alertly caught a fleeting glimpse of a strange ship and moved to investigate. As the British destroyer approached at 09:15, *Friedrich Eckoldt* opened fire. However, Kummetz could not engage freely in the dim light and atrocious weather. He ordered *Friedrich Eckoldt* and two other destroyers to break off and close with the flagship. Then HMS *Onslow* (Captain Sherbrooke) met *Hipper* at 09:29 in a sudden clearing. The German heavy cruiser immediately opened fire on the destroyer. Captain Sherbrooke reacted swiftly and placed his ship and HMS *Orwell* between the German warships and the convoy. The British escorts would sell themselves dearly.

Then at 09:30, *Lützow* sighted the merchants. *Lützow and Hipper* now had the convoy in a vise. But with visibility almost zero, Captain Stange recalled his destroyers to the mother ship.

Kummetz signaled at 09:36 *"Am engaging enemy."* Intent listeners in Hitler's HQ heard the message with great satisfaction. As the action developed HMS *Onslow* took a heavy hit at 10:19 and retired behind smoke. But HMS *Obedient* immediately took her place.

Later, at 10:45 *Lützow* again contacted the convoy - through snow squalls. But, relying totally on radar, Stange would not risk engaging his ships. Even strong radar echoes to port did not entice him to change course toward the convoy. Consequently, *Lützow* and her destroyers crossed the head of the merchants. *Lützow and Hipper* now sailed on the same side of the convoy - Kummetz's planned pincer tactic faded away.

Still engaged in action, Kummetz signaled at 11:32: *"Engaging close escorts. No cruisers."* The listening audience in the Wolfsschanze smiled confidently. Expectations mounted when U-354 reported a red glow in the sky. It seemed the situation had climaxed successfully.

Unfortunately for Kummetz, the situation had reversed. Two heavy cruisers, HMS *Sheffield* and HMS *Jamaica*, appeared like wraiths through the squalling mists. Equipped with radar-guided guns they opened fire on *Hipper*. Quickly they damaged a boiler room and set a blazing fire in *Hipper's* aircraft hanger. At this critical moment a warning signal arrived from SKL: *"Take no unnecessary risks. Use discretion against enemy of equal strength."* Extreme caution suggested Kummetz turn away and retire westwards.

At 12:03 he ordered *Lützow* and all ships to cease fire and withdraw. This came too late for *Friedrich Eckoldt*. She had damaged HMS *Obdurate* in their duel but went down at 11:34 with all hands. Kummetz sent a short, curt wireless signal, *"breaking off."* Then he sank into radio silence to evade pursuers. *Hipper* arrived at Altenfjord at 07:00 New Years Day - without reporting further details of the mission.

Chancellor Hitler had closed out 1942 with a New Year's Eve party in the Wolfsschanze. Although saturated with troubles from the eastern front, he seemed animated. The Führer bragged expansively to everyone about a wonderful naval success in the Arctic. As the evening advanced without further information, Hitler ordered Vice Admiral Kranke to get an update. An attempted wireless contact with Kummetz drew a blank. Furthermore, teleprinter services in Norway were broken down. No one could raise Kummetz.

Hitler's anxiety rose a notch when a Reuters report claimed British warships had thwarted an attack on an Arctic convoy. Reuters gave no details except that German losses included a destroyer sunk and a cruiser damaged. Hitler fumed but could not root out anything more about Kummetz's mission. In the afternoon 1 January, a detailed report arrived on the Führer's desk.

Hitler blasted Raeder's in house representative at the evening situation conference in the Wolfsschanze. Vice Admiral Kranke listened to Hitler ranting about the supreme commander getting information 24-hours after an action. The Führer raved with his customary criticisms: he berated the 'useless battleships' and the 'lack of daring' of the older officers. Then he ordered Kranke to inform the Admiralty that it was his unalterable resolve to pay off the heavy ships. "They were a needless drain of men and materials." . . . "It was time to reduce them to scrap and mount their guns on land installations." Hitler insisted that the official war diary record his views. Finally, he ordered Kranke to phone Raeder and instruct the grand admiral to come immediately to the Wolfsschanze.

Admiral Raeder pleaded illness to gain a little time but finally appeared at Rastenburg on 7 January. Hitler instantly tore into a ninety-minute tirade. With Field Marshal Keitel present, he revisited all the complaints that Raeder had suffered for years. Then Hitler repeated his unalterable intention to scrap the heavy ships. Grand Admiral Erich Raeder's life's work had slowly disintegrated over the last years. Now it crashed down around his shoulders.

Raeder listened passively to the full measure of Hitler's rage in silence. When the Führer's wrath finally petered out, Raeder requested a private audience. Admiral Raeder grimly asked Hitler to relieve him from his position as C-in-C navy. Hitler tried to backpedal from the heavy-ship issue. He complimented Raeder on the brilliant work of the submarines and light forces. But Raeder would not budge from his decision to resign. To lighten the political impact, Raeder offered to date his resignation 30 January 1943. This coincided with the tenth anniversary of the Third Reich. It would mark a natural transition from the old guard to a younger man.

At Hitler's request, Raeder wrote a detailed memo supporting the need for capital warships in Germany's operational fleet. The grand admiral recalled that war arrived five years too soon and wrecked the Z-Plan program. Raeder bitterly complained about the lack of cooperation from Göring's Luftwaffe. They did not provide sufficient aircraft for reconnaissance or naval air cover. Also, the fading possibility of ever getting an aircraft carrier measured greatly in Raeder's diatribe.

Ironically, Admiral Raeder blamed the Führer's policy of 'not taking risks' had stopped the heavy ships from fighting as their admirals had wished.

Raeder's memorandum did not impress Hitler. Grand Admiral Dr. Erich Raeder stepped down as Supreme Commander of the *Kriegsmarine* on Saturday 30 January 1943. Admiral Karl Dönitz, commander of the U-boats, moved into his place, including a promotion to grand admiral. It seemed the 'sacred cause' of a German world class surface fleet had run its course.

CHAPTER 23:
Grand Admiral Dönitz.

Admiral Karl Dönitz first met Adolf Hitler at a Führer naval conference in May 1942. U-boats had scored enormous successes and drawn Hitler's applause. Dönitz immediately fell under the influence of Hitler's dynamic personality. He valued Hitler's amazing powers of persuasion. The Führer invariably overcame any opposition from a complainant. On 25 January 1943, Dönitz received Hitler's battleship directive at the Wolfsschanze:

1. *All construction and conversion of heavy ships will cease with immediate effect....*
2. *Battleships, pocket-battleships, heavy cruisers and light cruisers are to be paid off, except where they are required for training purposes....*
3. *The surplus dockyard capacity resulting from this is to be applied to an intensification of U-boat repair and construction.*

Dönitz recognized the utter waste in Hitler's 'irrevocable' orders to scrap the heavy ships. These warships could play an important strategic role in waging an all-out submarine war. Furthermore, it suited Dönitz if powerful old guard officers in Raeder's corner gave their full support to the new C-in-C.

Three weeks later - 8 February - Dönitz carefully proposed that *Tirpitz* and *Scharnhorst* might remain in 'temporary' service as 'mobile batteries.' *Lützow* and *Admiral Scheer* would continue as 'training vessels.' In keeping with Hitler's directive, the navy would 'slowly' pay off *Hipper, Leipzig and Köln.* Hitler accepted Dönitz's delaying strategy with a dismissive shrug.

At a conference with Hitler on 26 February, Dönitz advanced the idea of reenlisting the heavy ships. He argued that the navy needed a northern battle group to counter the worsening situation on the Russian front. Dönitz suggested *Scharnhorst* should join *Tirpitz* in Norway. Hitler pouted angrily and remarked on the dismal performance of the heavy ships to date. Dönitz patiently countered. He pointed to the restrictive orders that had compelled the ships' commanders to 'tread carefully and remain afloat.' Hitler snapped, "If our ships meet the enemy they must fight." Dönitz moved quickly to the offensive. "Then, *mein Führer*, I may send *Scharnhorst* to Norway?" Hitler remained disgruntled but conceded the point. *Scharnhorst* subsequently joined *Tirpitz* and *Lützow* at Narvik 14 March 1943. Battle Group 1 under Rear Admiral Kummetz then moved to Altenfjord and awaited orders.

Kummetz saved his battle group's low allocations of fuel oil and waited for a call to action. An accidental explosion on 8 April caused anxieties for *Scharnhorst*. Ammunition in the after turret magazine exploded and killed seventeen crew members. Through the summer tradesmen worked to repair the damage.

Initially, Kummetz took out his battle group to raid Spitzbergen on 8 September. They landed troops to blow up installations while the heavy ships bombarded Longyearbyen, Barentsburg and Sveagruvafjord. It proved a successful training mission. The German warships returned to their lair in Altenfjord before the British could counter.

Britain had now suspended summer convoys to Russia. Supporting the allied landings in North Africa superseded Stalin's aggressive demands. Besides, winter convoys had achieved better success. Admiralty interest in the German battle group now focused on new tactics and weapons. Heavy bombers could not find suitable facilities in Russia. The current Home Fleet had only one old aircraft carrier - HMS *Furious* - that could not deliver a major strike. Meanwhile, *Tirpitz* deterred full convoy resumption with her powerful presence in the Arctic.

British ingenuity and resourcefulness prevailed. They sent a small group of midget submarines on a highly dangerous sortie. Operation *Source* made a successful attack on *Tirpitz* at Kaafjord on 22 September. Two tiny X-craft submarines, with two men in each, passed the nets protecting *Tirpitz* and laid limpet mines on her hull. Two horrendous explosions smashed the port rudder and jammed all three propellers. Powerful blasts disabled both Anton and Caesar turrets. *Tirpitz* could not move under her own power.

Although both X-craft were forced to the surface, the captured British sailors received good treatment. Miraculously, *Tirpitz* survived without sinking but faced months of repair work. The navy rejected a hazardous towing operation to Kiel or Wilhelmshaven. Preferably, they brought in 800 repair technicians to work on *Tirpitz* at Kaafjord.

Lützow had now returned to Gdynia for refit. Kummetz's Battle Group 1 had diminished to *Scharnhorst* and five destroyers. Rear Admiral Kummetz took 'indefinite sick leave' and returned to Germany. Rear Admiral Erich Bey replaced Kummetz as C-in-C of the battle group. A dashing, spirited officer, 'Achmed' Bey had held the position of Flag Officer Destroyers.

British intelligence thankfully noted the decrease of the German battle group. *Scharnhorst* remained the only capital ship to threaten Russian convoys. They decided to open the convoys and set a trap for the battle cruiser. Admiral Bruce Fraser, newly appointed C-in-C of the Home Fleet, believed the Germans would attack the convoys with vigor. Fraser felt confident, with the help of Ultra intercepts and advanced radar technology, he could wipe out the *Scharnhorst*.

At the end of October British warships escorted the first convoy of empty merchant ships from Archangel to Britain. Convoy RA-54A arrived unmolested. Then on 15 November JW-54A, eighteen merchants loaded with war supplies, left Loch Ewe. The second half of the eastbound convoy, JW-54B, followed a week later. Both arrived without incident in Russia.

Admiral Fraser provided 'full trip' battleship coverage with the *Duke of York* for the next convoy. He expected a German raiding sortie anytime. JW-55A with nineteen merchants, sailed from Loch Ewe on 12 December and arrived safely in Archangel ten days later. Fraser's flagship had quickly refueled in Iceland and returned to shepherd JW-55B.

Admiral Dönitz met Hitler on 20 December - the same day that JW-55B left Loch Ewe. The Führer and the generals lamented the serious deterioration on the Russian front and the continuing success of British convoys. Dönitz offered to attack the first vulnerable convoy with *Scharnhorst* and the rest of the destroyers in Battle Group 1. Hitler concurred, with limited expectations of a successful raid.

The British Admiralty now raised the stakes and organized a

convoy of empties (RA-55A) to sail from Murmansk on 22 December. Both convoys, RA-55A, westbound, and JW-55B, eastbound, would get close escort coverage with battleship and cruiser backup. Fraser divided his backup into two groups. Heavy cruisers under Rear Admiral Burnett would cover the west-bound empties (RA-55A) to Bear Island. Burnett would then escort the eastbound convoy (JW-55B) back to Russia. Fraser's battleship with *Jamaica* and four destroyers would take JW-55B to Bear Island then patrol in the North Cape area. *Duke of York's* 14-inch guns would punish *Scharnhorst* if she dared to appear.

On 22 December, a patrolling Luftwaffe aircraft sighted JW-55B off the Faeroes. Admiral Schniewind, now C-in-C Naval Group North, ordered all eight U-boats in the Arctic to the Bear Island passage. Simultaneously, he telegraphed an order to Rear Admiral Bey to raise steam for three hours' notice. Luftwaffe aircraft continued surveillance and reported the convoy on 24 December advancing eastward, 500-miles south east of Jan Mayen Island.

Schniewind did not know that RA-55A was steaming westward with cruiser backup. Also, German surveillance did not pick up *Duke of York* racing at full speed to close the Bear Island passage. To compound Schniewind's problems, the Fifth *Luftflotte* H.Q. in Oslo informed him that strike aircraft were not available. Furthermore, they could not guarantee continued reconnaissance unless the navy 'confirmed a firm intent' of launching a surface attack on the convoy. With Christmas Day approaching, the aircrews no doubt wanted relief.

Alarm signals vibrated through Schniewind's mind. Long experienced in Luftwaffe reticence in helping the navy, he decided to advise Dönitz to abort the intended sortie. His phone call to Berlin revealed that Dönitz had gone to Paris. All decisions must wait his return in twenty-four hours. At 14:15 on Christmas Day, Dönitz reaffirmed the sortie and issued an executive order to launch Operation *Ostfront*. Within minutes, Schniewind's group in Kiel forwarded orders to Rear Admiral Bey - sail at 17:00. Bey's orders included a restatement of new OKM policy: *"Tactical situation to be exploited skillfully and boldly. Engagement not to be broken off until full success achieved. . . Scharnhorst's superior fire power is crucial. . . Disengage at own discretion, and automatically if heavy forces are encountered."* Dönitz had earlier decreed that fleet commanders must have complete freedom of action without interference from Naval

Group North. Consequently, Rear Admiral Bey's orders carried an adventurous tone of 'sink or swim'. 'Achmed' Bey had planned to keep *Scharnhorst* in a backup role to a destroyer attack. Now he revised his plans, deciding to lead boldly with his flag-ship.

Inefficient Luftwaffe reconnaissance and B-Dienst monitoring left Schniewind without knowledge of Burnett's cruisers steaming eastward. Fraser's *Duke of York* now covered Bear Island - unobserved. Luftwaffe H.Q. then cancelled all reconnaissance flights for 26 December, citing bad weather.

Schniewind hastily phoned Dönitz to cancel Operation *Ostfront* but Dönitz refused. Later, at 02:06 Schniewind sent a telegram to again request cancellation of the *Scharnhorst* sortie. But Dönitz had promised Hitler an all-out attempt. Again he refused to cancel. The navy must overcome the Führer's intolerance of the big ships' seeming reluctance to fight.

Flying into atrocious weather, six flying boats manned by *Kriegsmarine* volunteers, took off in early morning 26 December. Heading into the Arctic, one machine encountered radar signals at 10:12, emanating from *Duke of York*. The pilot reported sighting a large ship plus some smaller vessels in the area. This report did not arrive in Narvik until 13:41. Two hours later they passed the signal to Rear Admiral Bey but dropped the reference to 'one large ship'. B-Dienst also reported unusual volumes of enemy wireless traffic which they could not read. They interpreted this as a possible heavy covering force heading for *Scharnhorst*. Incredibly, Schniewind's staff at Naval Group North did not pass this information to *Scharnhorst*. They assessed the information as too vague.

At 07:00 on 26 December, Rear Admiral Bey fanned out his destroyers in search of the convoy. Sailing southwesterly, he knew when HMS *Belfast* picked up *Scharnhorst* on radar at 08:40. Burnett's cruisers steadily closed the range. At 09:21 HMS *Norfolk* opened fire with an 8-inch volley. Bey immediately swung his ship south, then reversed to steer north at full speed. *Scharnhorst* ran out of the enemy radar range but the cruisers continued their search.

They recovered *Scharnhorst* on radar at 12:05. Gunfire exchanges left *Norfolk* damaged, but Bey could not shake off the British radar pursuit. Now steering at maximum speed on course SSW, he unwittingly sped toward *Duke of York*. Rear Admiral Bey had a strong premonition of disaster. He released his destroyers to return to Altenfjord.

At 16:17 Bey's premonition took form when *Duke of York's* radar displayed the German battle cruiser - range 22 miles. At 16:50 a star shell lit up *Scharnhorst* like a stage floodlight. Radar-directed 14-inch shells soon pounded into the luckless German. HMS *Jamaica* joined the attack and *Scharnhorst* replied with her 11-inch volleys. Turning and weaving ferociously like a wolf at bay, the battle cruiser could not escape the murderous 14-inch volleys from *Duke of York*. Captain Hintze, Bey's flag captain, ordered the flooding of his forward powder store to contain a flash fire. About 18:20, in arctic darkness, a hit in No. 1 boiler room temporarily reduced *Scharnhorst's* speed to 10 knots. When she regained speed to 20 knots, the cruisers and destroyers of Fraser's back-up force had joined the fray.

Captain Hintze (flag captain) bravely sent a final signal, *"We shall fight to the last shell."* At 19:45 *Scharnhorst* lay ablaze - a blackened mass of twisted metal. A sudden earthshaking explosion sent shimmering pieces of debris toward the sky. When the echoes settled, *Scharnhorst* had disappeared. Rear Admiral Bey and Captain Hintze went down with most of the ship's complement - 1,968 souls. Only thirty-six survivors remained.

Admiral Dönitz distanced himself from the loss of *Scharnhorst*. He credited the British victory to superior radar technology. The Führer expressed further discontent with the failure of the big ships to stand and fight. "As in the *Graf Spee,* they give too much thought to protecting our big ships." Hitler blamed Rear Admiral Bey for running away from cruisers that he could overpower. Luftwaffe and administrative carelessness escaped scrutiny or censure.

The year 1943 passed and tilted the outcome of the war toward an allied victory. Although German shipyards produced more than 300 U-boats in 1942, they arrived too late. Stunning allied shipping losses off the American coast during 1942 resulted in an acceleration of counter-measures. Ultra signals interception and improved radar now found the lurking U-boats. Small, specially equipped antisubmarine vessels and aircraft attacked the wolf–packs. Improved range helped land-based aircraft to root out U-boats in the center of the Atlantic. And new ships and equipment streamed off the American and British production lines in ever increasing numbers.

Beginning in the middle of November 1942, British bombers hammered German production centers and cities every night. American Flying Fortresses soon contributed with daylight raids. One thousand bombers dropping high explosives from 30,000 feet onto the factories and the families created chaos. As Germany's war production faltered allied materials multiplied. Allied troop landings in Algeria and Morocco in November 1942 turned the desert war into a European invasion opportunity. In 1943, successful allied landings in Sicily soon expanded to the Italian mainland. Fierce fighting steadily pressed German defenses northward through Italy. On the Eastern front, Russian counter offenses swept huge pockets of desperate German troops into death or surrender. Meanwhile, allied forces built up a powerful invasion army in Britain. They crossed the English Channel into France on 6 June 1944. Huge convoys brought an uninterrupted river of supplies to the allied advance.

Still, one German capital ship occupied the attention of the British Admiralty. Special teams of Barracuda dive bombers had practiced maneuvers to finish off *Tirpitz*. Fleet Air Arm carrier planes managed to inflict damage with 1600-pound bombs during August but could not sink the German warship. The Admiralty passed the *Tirpitz* problem to the Royal Air Force.

Lancaster bombers flew over Kaafjord on 11 September. They dropped 6-ton monster bombs from 12,000 feet into a smoke-screened target area. *Tirpitz* took enormous damage but remained afloat. Captain Wolfe Junge submitted an urgent report to Dönitz suggesting removal of *Tirpitz* from the active list. Admiral Dönitz stubbornly refused and ordered the ship moved to Tromsö - 200 miles south.

Repair gangs worked frantically on the ship and on 10 October *Tirpitz* steamed at a snail's pace through the Leads to Tromsö. A berth in the lee of Haakoy Island provided a defensive situation. Shallow water assured the ship would not sink below her turrets. At worst they could use her 15-inch guns as fixed batteries. Additionally, two flak ships moved into the fjord, adding further strength to smoke defenses.

On 4 November former gunnery officer Robert Weber replaced Captain Junge as commander of *Tirpitz*. Unfortunately for *Tirpitz*, Tromsö came within the range of the Lancaster Bomber Base at

Lossiemouth, Scotland. Each plane could carry a 6-ton 'tall boy' bomb. On 12 November a determined Lancaster bomber attack finished *Tirpitz*. Despite a furious anti-aircraft response from all her guns, she took deadly punishment and capsized. Captain Weber and 700 crew members lost their lives.

Germany now had her back against the wall. Hitler had demanded 10,000 sailors to help the *Wehrmacht* at the Russian front. Dönitz did not have the naval strength to disrupt the English Channel beach heads. Nonetheless, every available small warship including E-boats and 'Biber' one-man submarines perpetually harassed the allied landings.

Biber submarines carried two torpedoes or one mine and one torpedo. They often leaked carbon monoxide fumes into the cramped, one-man cockpit. In an ironic twist of fate Lieutenant Jochen Langsdorff lost his life on 20 December 1944 in a Biber attack. The *Graf Spee's* captain's son went missing on the anniversary date of his father's suicide.

Hitler had now belatedly agreed that the 'training vessels' *Lützow* and *Admiral Scheer* could form a battle group in the Baltic. The pocket battleships joined with *Prinz Eugen* and *Hipper* to form Battle Group 2. Vice Admiral August Thiele commanded the group. At the end of November Soviet troops had overwhelmed *Wehrmacht* defenses at the Sorve Peninsula. General Guderian organized an evacuation operation. Despite constant aircraft and submarine attacks, Thiele's battle group accomplished heroic service in moving troops and civilians through the Baltic. As the vengeful Soviet armies churned westward, Thiele's ships bombarded the Soviet flank along the Baltic.

On 20 January 1945, the Soviet avalanche broke through on a 50-mile front in East Prussia. The German retreat collapsed into a rout. *Admiral Scheer* scooped up 800 refugees and 200 wounded soldiers from Gdynia and headed for Kiel. *Scheer's* gun barrels were worn smooth from constant action. A few days later - 27 March - Soviet advance troops seized Gdynia.

At Kiel the armored cruiser received a stopgap coat of violet-blue paint to 'spruce her up' for a visit from Admiral Schniewind. Despite a moment of humorous relief, sustained attacks from Lancaster bombers sank the ex-pocket battleship at her berth on 10 April. The heavy cruiser *Hipper* also took severe damage from the Lancaster bombers.

Fatefully, the first battleship to initiate the Z-Plan now carried the lead role in the ruptured plan's end. *Lützow*, formerly *Deutschland*, remained the only heavy ship in the German navy. *Lützow* had covered the retreat of Kummetz's armada of assorted vessels taking troops and refugees from the Hela Peninsula. Constantly fighting off aircraft and submarine attacks, she courageously earned her stripes in the final days of the war. Running low on fuel and ammunition, *Lützow* finally retreated to Sweinemünde.

Like baying hounds the Lancaster bombers sniffed her out and ended her sailing days. Listing to port, she settled into the shallows of the *Kaiserfahrt* Canal, her main turrets still above the surface. Amazingly, the ex-pocket battleship soon took her place as a heavy artillery battery. On 27 April, as the Soviets advanced toward Pasewalk, she again went into action. Patched and lying level on the sand-filled bottom, she opened fire with her forward 11-inch and four medium guns. *Lützow* continued to fight until an electrical fire silenced her main guns. At 00:12 on 4 May 1945, a demolition crew blew her up. Thirty hours later the European war ended with a declaration of unconditional surrender.

The End of the Road.

CHAPTER 24:

Unconditional Surrender.

Hitler's military successes in the Second World War reached an apex in summer 1942. Most of Europe lay under Nazi control or maintained a neutral posture. German submarines in the Atlantic sank more than 900 merchant ships for a total exceeding 6,250,000 tons. General Rommel's *Afrika Korps* captured Tobruk in June 1942 and advanced to El Alamein - 65 miles from Alexandria. Field Marshal Kesselring's Luftwaffe, flying from land bases, virtually controlled the Mediterranean basin. Then the tide turned.

In the Battle of the Atlantic, the United States' entry into the war helped stem the disastrous shipping losses. The allied camp quickly put together a potent antisubmarine defense. Large convoys of merchant ships successfully moved enough vital supplies to sustain the turn around. U-boat effectiveness tapered off in 1943.

During 1942, Malta reeled under horrendous bombing but survived. Fortress Malta played a key role in the allies offensive in the Mediterranean. General Auchinleck's Eighth Army skillfully retreated from Tobruk then held fast at El Alamein. In October 1942, General Montgomery (Auchinleck's successor) broke out of El Alamein. The Eighth Army's westward advance recaptured air bases in Cyrenaica and eased the pressure in the Mediterranean.

In 1943, allied forces cleared all German resistance out of the Mediterranean coastline in North Africa. From this vantage point they soon invaded Sicily and hedge hopped into Italy. During 1944, allied troops advanced slowly but relentlessly through Italy.

Hitler's unswerving will to defeat the Soviet Union had concentrated the German war effort on the Eastern front. But Stalingrad obstinately held out and the German advance into the Caucasus ran out of steam. On 19 November 1942, the Soviet armies began a massive counter offensive that pushed the Germans back from Stalingrad. The Red Army encircled twenty-two German divisions between the River Volga and the River Don. Adolf Hitler's orders to the front betrayed his manic drive to defeat the Soviets. Retreat was not an option. The army must succeed or die in the field. Hitler would consider any retreat cowardly or traitorous.

Finally in 1944, Hitler's hands-on direction of the army inspired an extreme reaction. Some high level military officers conspired to assassinate the Führer. On 20 July, Count von Stauffenberg placed a powerful time-bomb close to Hitler at the Wolfsschanze. The resultant explosion shook the whole complex. Stauffenberg then rushed to Berlin to meet the conspirators. General Beck, General Goerdeler and Field Marshal von Witzleben would form a new government and negotiate peace terms.

However, the plot fizzled out when Hitler stumbled out of the conference room, bedraggled but very much alive. A subsequent police round–up of suspects ended in unparalleled cruelty and executions. Admiral Raeder had remained in limbo since his resignation. Hitler had given him the title of Inspector General of the Navy - without any official function. Nonetheless, rebellion against the state found no place in Raeder's psyche. The admiral immediately visited the Führer to show his continuing loyalty. Raeder escaped any Gestapo molestation but they imprisoned and tortured his old friend, former Minister of Defense Otto Gessler.

Hitler's personal control of the military had aroused bitter dissent among the generals - but he held on. The Führer had rock hard faith that Providence would hand him a final victory. Meanwhile, suspicions of treachery within the ranks increased daily. Hitler resorted to multiple medications to counteract his failing health.

As 1945 approached, a relative stand-off on all fronts allowed Hitler to review the war situation. Despite unceasing allied bombing attacks, Albert Speer, the minister for war supplies, had delivered an incredible increase in war essentials. Only tank production fell short of the previous year's figures. However, oil and gasoline supplies formed a stress point in the war effort. Constant allied bombing of fuel plants had left Germany only five weeks of aircraft fuel in reserve.

Reaching for a miracle, the Führer had an inspiration - he proposed a new western offensive. Hitler believed a surprise attack into the Ardennes and Alsace could recapture Antwerp. If successful, Germany might gain breathing space to regroup and bring new weapons on stream. Concurrently, he foresaw a split in the allied hierarchy because of conflicting philosophies. Communist Soviet Russia and the capitalistic West made uncomfortable partners.

Hitler's generals opposed this strategic change in the war. All agreed that a surprise offensive might deal a heavy blow. But given shorter supply lines, the allies would rapidly reinforce the new front and frustrate the main objective. Driving all available reserves into a concentrated push against the west could only help a new Soviet offensive. Hitler overruled these negative premises.

On 16 December, German armored divisions launched a surprise attack against the Western front. They gained ground quickly in the first week but soon ran into insurmountable defenses. Meanwhile, General Guderian implored Hitler to strengthen the weakened Eastern front. Hitler refused until 8 January - then he agreed to divert armor from the Ardennes: Too late to staunch a massive Soviet offensive.

The Red Army opened its attack in Poland on 12 January. German defenses crumpled before one-hundred-eighty Soviet divisions storming across the Baltic-Carpathians line. The death's knell of Hitler's Third Reich began to toll. Within three months the fighting fronts closed around Germany, leaving a one-hundred-mile-wide corridor running through the Fatherland. As the victorious allies gained ground on all fronts, a change in Washington gave Hitler a glimmer of hope. President Roosevelt lost his fight against ailing health. Roosevelt died on 12 April 1945 and Harry Truman moved into the White House. Hitler imagined the changeover might alter allied policy but it did not.

Adolf Hitler turned 56 years old on 20 April. The Führer gathered his henchmen in the Reich Chancellery to mourn rather than celebrate his birthday. Göring, Himmler, Goebbels, Ribbentrop, Bormann and Speer with the chiefs of the armed services listened to Hitler's final plans. It boiled down to splitting Germany into a Northern and Southern Command. Grand Admiral Dönitz would command the north. Field Marshal Kesselring already commanded the south. A last-ditch command post at Berchtesgaden offered a final redoubt from the approaching Soviets. Hitler had decided to hold on in Berlin, but anyone could leave for the south if they wished. Goebbels and Bormann remained with Hitler in Berlin through the final days.

On 23 April, Hermann Göring sent a wireless message to Hitler. Göring quoted a 1941 decree - in case of succession - that gave him authority over the party and the nation. Martin Bormann immediately stifled Göring's attempt to succeed Hitler. Instead he prompted Hitler into cancelling Göring's Nazi party and military credentials. The Führer accused the field marshal of treason and ordered Göring arrested.

Heinrich Himmler also harbored thoughts of succeeding Hitler. He approached Count Bernadotte at the Swedish embassy with an idea to negotiate peace. Himmler suggested a peace accord that excluded the Soviet Union. The allies immediately shunned this idea. Hitler caught wind of Himmler's actions and the SS chief joined Göring on the outcast list.

Hitler now decided to end his life - Russian shells were dropping around the Chancellery. At 04:00 Sunday 29 April, he signed his last testament. Hitler chose Grand Admiral Dönitz to succeed him as president and supreme head of the armed forces. Josef Goebbels would take the chancellor position and Martin Bormann the Nazi party ministry.

Adolf Hitler died from a self-inflicted gunshot in the head at 15:30 on 30 April. Beside him in his bunker lay the poisoned body of his longtime mistress. Hitler had married Eva Braun a few hours before her suicide. Martin Bormann immediately sent a wireless message to Grand Admiral Dönitz. It advised Dönitz of his new responsibilities: President of the Reich and supreme commander of the armed forces.

Dönitz recognized that negotiating peace must take top priority in his new position. Calmly and quickly, he set up a provisional government in the naval academy at Flensburg-Mürwik. They carefully excluded high profile, unsavory Nazis. Heinrich Himmler lobbied for a position but received a rebuttal.

Dönitz selected General Admiral von Friedeburg as his personal envoy to open discussions with the allies. However, evacuation operations ahead of the ferocious Soviet Armies continued in the Baltic. Dönitz gave Friedeburg instructions to offer a partial surrender that might allow the ongoing rescue of refugees. Field Marshal Montgomery seemed ready to allow some leeway in these circumstances. But General Eisenhower, the allied supreme commander, wanted an unconditional surrender on all fronts. Friedeburg persisted, and arranged a partial surrender of the German forces facing Montgomery's troops. With Montgomery's accord, German destroyers and e-boats left port in a desperate attempt to pick up refugees from the Hela Peninsula. They succeeded in evacuating 43,000 people.

After almost six years of horrendous carnage, the Second World War in Europe ended abruptly on 8 May 1945. Germany, her military back broken, signed a declaration of unconditional surrender.

Less than three months later - 6 August - an atomic bomb demolished Hiroshima, killing at least fifty thousand Japanese civilians. United States President Harry Truman then authorized a second nuclear strike against Japan. Nagasaki fell in ruins on 14 August and Japan surrendered unconditionally on 21 August 1945.

Around the world, the balm of peace began to ease the aching wounds left from six years of devastation.

CHAPTER 25:

Kriegsmarine on Trial.

At the height of hostilities in the Second World War, delegates from nine occupied European countries met in London. In January 1942, they resolved to punish war criminals, including the instigators. Great Britain, the United States and the Soviet Union approved the St. James Declaration.

At Casablanca, in January 1943, President Roosevelt broached the subject of war crimes with Prime Minister Churchill. After the meeting Roosevelt asked Henry Stimson, secretary of war, and Cordell Hull, secretary of state, to submit their views on the matter. This led to the United Nations War Crimes Commission (UNWCC), set up in 1943.

Henry Stimson held very strong ideas: Prosecute and severely punish war criminals but rehabilitate the German nation after the war. Henry Morgenthau, secretary of the treasury, totally opposed this notion. He believed they should summarily execute war criminals and reduce Germany's economy to a subsistence level: "they should turn Germany into a pastoral wasteland." Nevertheless, at Roosevelt's request, Cordell Hull and Henry Stimson prepared an American plan for the president.

Under the direction of Assistant Secretary of War John McCloy, the Special Projects Branch of the War Office produced a six-page brief. It dismissed Morgenthau's idea for summary executions as un-American. Colonel Murray C. Bernays, the architect of McCloy's plan, had taken Stimson's principal concerns and filled in some necessary details. Foremost in his brief, Bernays proposed that 'unconditional surrender' could form the basis for an international military tribunal.

Roosevelt and Churchill met in Quebec, Canada from 11 until 19 September 1944. Morgenthau attended the meeting to cover any financial issues. He seized this opportunity to present his bloodthirsty plan for post-war handling of war criminals. Churchill and Roosevelt initialed the plan, intending to get Stalin's opinion at an upcoming meeting in Yalta. However, Morgenthau's draconian opinions leaked to the American press. It caused an angry political explosion in the United States.

At Yalta on 22 January 1945, the allied leaders discussed a memorandum from Stimson, Hull and Francis Biddle, the American attorney general. It recommended a military tribunal to try Nazi leaders for atrocious crimes. The indictment included a conspiracy to commit crimes against German citizens during the war - and before it began. Roosevelt and Stalin favored a military trial, and Churchill reluctantly joined them in issuing a joint declaration. This led to the international military tribunal at Nuremberg.

In August 1945, the allies identified twenty-four Nazi candidates for prosecution. Hitler and Goebbels were considered dead but they included Martin Bormann in absentia. The Russians had added Admiral Raeder and Hans Fritzsche to the list while the Americans had always included Admiral Dönitz. Both allies overruled the British preference not to try either admiral.

On Monday, 30 September 1946, after ten months of grueling hearings the tribunal announced their judgement. Twenty-one men, who represented the highest ranks of Hitler's Nazi era, awaited their fate. They sat on two long, wooden pews in the Palace of Justice. The crowded court-room had heard elaborate arguments detailing incredible evil and barbarity before and during the war. Now, the top echelons who held civil and military power during Hitler's heyday, would bear responsibility for alleged crimes. Hitler's Nazi regime was on trial. The court considered four major counts:

1. Conspiracy and Planning to Precipitate Aggressive War.
2. War Crimes.
3. Crimes Against Humanity.
4. Crimes Against Peace.

Huddled side by side in the front bench sat the accused: Hermann Göring, Rudolf Hess, Joachim von Ribbentrop, Wilhelm Keitel, Ernst

Kaltenbrunner, Alfred Rosenberg, Hans Frank, Wilhelm Frick, Julius Streicher, Walther Funk and Hjalmar Schacht. Behind them, seated on a second bench, another row of defendants waited expectantly: Karl Dönitz, Erich Raeder, Baldur von Schirach, Fritz Sauckel, Alfred Jodl, Franz von Papen, Arthur Seyss-Inquart, Albert Speer, Constantin von Neurath and Hans Fritzsche. Some high profile names on the allied lists did not face the court: Adolf Hitler and Josef Goebbels had committed suicide in the chancellery as the Russians overran Berlin. Heinrich Himmler, captured and detained by British forces, had subsequently committed suicide. Robert Ley had ingeniously strangled himself in his prison holding cell before the trial.

Rendering of verdicts lasted until 13:35. Each man heard his name called, then listened to the verdict of the court. The judges acquitted Schacht, von Papen and Fritzsche before they broke for a recess. In the afternoon session, the guards individually escorted each guilty prisoner to the dock to face the bench. A dramatic hush silenced the crammed court-room as the judges read each sentence. Dönitz, von Schirach, Speer and von Neurath received prison terms ranging from ten to twenty years. They convicted Hess, Funk and Raeder to life in prison. Then they sentenced the remaining eleven prisoners to death by hanging. Hermann Göring had brazenly strutted and battled his way through the long trial. Having failed to avoid the death sentence, he ended his life with concealed cyanide pills, hours before his execution.

Grand Admiral Raeder's original shock when charged as a war criminal had changed to passive acceptance. The court found him guilty. Raeder expected to face a firing squad - an acceptable end to a long honorable military career. His sentence to life imprisonment desolated the admiral. He immediately asked the court to put him before a firing squad. The judges refused this request and Grand Admiral Raeder faced spending his old age in prison.

Charges of war crimes also stunned Grand Admiral Dönitz. His military contribution to the war had centered in the submarine program. Without question, Dönitz's U-boat strategy and tactics had sunk many merchant ships without warning. Dönitz's lawyer, Captain Otto Kranzbuehler, conspicuously dressed in his German naval uniform, produced a testimonial from US Admiral Chester Nimitz. It confirmed that the US navy had used 'unrestricted' submarine warfare since entering the war. Kranzbuehler argued convincingly that the German navy had fought a 'clean' fight. Grand Admiral Dönitz felt vindicated. Still, the tribunal gave him ten years in prison.

Admiral Dönitz served his full ten-year punishment and Admiral Raeder served ten years in Spandau before his early release. These highest level naval officers had promoted widely divergent ideas of a German naval force during their careers. But their differences remained moot after the war. Both grand admirals revered the German navy's war record. Together, in harmony they lobbied for a prominent naval force in Germany's military future. The *Kriegsmarine* dream had turned full circle.

Grand Admiral Raeder and Grand Admiral Dönitz (1957)   — GIESSLER

Cairo 1942. Rear Admiral Harwood at Churchill Conference — Harwood Family

British diver explores Graf Spee *in Montevideo (1940) Trocadero*

Vice Admiral Sir Henry Harwood KCB., OBE

Commanders Klepp, Ascher and Wattenberg in Buenos Aires

– JOSEPH GILBEY

Graf Spee *crew arrives in Buenos Aires* — RASENACK

*Captain Woodhouse DSC., (Ajax) and Captain Bell DSC., (Exeter) in London
(1940)* — HARWOOD FAMILY

Captain Langsdorff and Herr Otto Langmann in Montevideo

— JOSEPH GILBEY

Admiral Graf Spee *in Montevideo* — WALSH

Graf Spee *scuttled off Montevideo* — JOSEPH GILBEY

Notes

Chapter 15:
1. Admiralty PG / 32025 NID

Chapter 16:
1. See map on pages four and five

Chapter 17:
1. Papers of Rear Admiral Walter C. Ansel (Box 10 folder 10) Old Dominion University Norfolk VA

Chapter 19:
1. & 2. Admiralty File PG / 32025 NID presented at Nuremberg Military Tribunal GB exibit 194 January 14, 1946

Chapter 20:
1. ADM 116/4472 Kew Gardens Archives

2. ADM 116/281/84 Kew gardens Archives

Bibliography

Andrew, Christopher, Secret Service; The Making of the British Intelligence
   Community,
   William Heinemann Ltd.., Great Britain (1985).
Breyer, Siegfried, Battleships and Battle Cruisers.
   (1905 - 1970)
Brown, Anthony Cave, ' C ' The Secret Life of Sir Stewart Graham Menzies.
   MacMillan Publishing Co. (1988).
Bullock, Allan, Hitler; A Study in Tyranny, Konecky and Konecky, New York
   (1962).
Churchill, Sir Winston S., The Gathering Storm, Houghton Mifflin Co., Boston
   (1948)
Churchill, Sir Winston S., The Hinge of Fate, Houghton Mifflin Co., Boston
   (1950).
Edwards, Bernard, Salvo! Classic Naval Gun Actions, Arms and Armour Press,
   London (1995).
Gilbey, Joseph, Langsdorff of the Graf Spee, Hillsburgh, Ontario, Canada
   (1999).
Graber, G.S., History of the SS, Robert Hale, London (1978)
Gray, Edwin, Hitler's Battleships, Leo Cooper, London (1992).
Grove. Eric J, The Price of Disobedience, Sutton Publishing, Stroud, England
   (2000).
Gurr, John A., In Peace and in War, Square One Publications, Worcester,
   England (1993).
Hadley, Michael L, and Roger Sarty, Tin-Pots and Pirate Ship, McGill- Queens
   University Press, Montreal P.Q. , Canada (1991).
Heiden, Konrad, The Führer, Robinson Publishing, London (1999)
Hitler, Adolf, Mein Kampf, Houghton Mifflin Co., Boston (1971) .
Hailey, Foster, and Milton Lancelot, Clear for Action, Duell, Sloan and Pearce,
   New York (1964).
Jane's Fighting Ships of World War II
   Bracken Books (1989)
James, Robert Rhodes, MP., Churchill Speaks 1897-1963, Chelsea House
   Publishers (1980),
Johns, W.E., and R.A. Kelly, No Surrender, W.H.Allen & Co., London (1969).
Manchester, Wm., The Last Lion (W.S. Churchill), Little Brown, Boston (1988).

Raeder, Eric, Grand Admiral, My Life, US Naval Institute, Annapolis, Maryland (1960).

Roper, Trevor, Hitler's War Directives 1939-1945, Pan Books, London (1964).

Reuth, George Ralf, Goebbels, Harcourt Brace, Florida (1993)

Sceptre; Hoddder and Stoughton Ltd (1987).

Sebag- Montefiore, Hugh, Enigma- The Battle for the Code, Orion House, London (2000).

Shankland, Peter, and Anthony Hunter, Malta Convoy, Collins, London (1961).

Shirir, William L., The Nightmare Years: 1930-1940, Little Brown, Boston (1984).

Showell, Jak P. Mallman, U-Boat Command and the Battle of the Atlantic, Vanwell Publishing, St. Catherines., Ontario, Canada (1989).

Showell, Jak P. Mallmann, The German Navy in World War II (1935 - 1945)

Tusa, The Nuremberg Trial
   Ann and John Tusa, MacMillan, London (1983)

Tuchmann, Barbara W., The Zimmermann Telegram, Constable & Co., London (1958).

Vian, Sir Philip L., Action This Day, Frederick Muller Ltd., London (1960).

Warner, Philip, Auchinleck - The Lonely Soldier, Sphere Books, London (1981).

Unpublished Materials:

Donat, Rudolf. Kriegstagbuch - *Panzerschiff Admiral Graf Spee* (Captain Langsdorff's log book printed and distributed privately in Germany 1993.)

Hill, M.C. Admiral Graf Spee, The daily diary of a seaman who served on HMS *Achilles* during the battle.

Index

About the Author

Joseph Gilbey is a freelance writer. Born in Scotland, he immigrated to Canada in 1957. On a visit to Montevideo in 1994 he became captivated with the unique story of Captain Hans Langsdorff who commanded *Admiral Graf Spee* in the Battle of the River Plate. Following five years of intensive, international research he published *'Langsdorff of the Graf Spee: Prince of Honor'*. This opened up further interest in the broader subject of the Kriegsmarine and the Z-Plan. Gilbey now connects the Kriegsmarine of the Second World War directly to the Kaiser's Imperial Navy. *'Kriegsmarine: Admiral Raeder's Navy'* is a fascinating story.